BIBLIOPHOBIA

BIBLIOPHOBIA

A MEMOIR

Sarah Chihaya

RANDOM HOUSE

NEW YORK

Published in the United States by Random House, an imprint and
division of Penguin Random House LLC, New York.

RANDOM HOUSE and the HOUSE colophon are
registered trademarks of Penguin Random House LLC.

Grateful acknowledgment is made to the following for permission
to reprint previously published material:

BJORK, ONE LITTLE INDEPENDENT RECORDS, KOBALT MUSIC PUBLISHING:
Excerpt from "Hyperballad" by Bjork. Used by permission.
NEW DIRECTIONS PUBLISHING CORP: Excerpts from "The Glass Essay" from
GLASS, IRONY, AND GOD by Anne Carson, copyright © 1995 by Anne Carson.
Reprinted by permission of New Directions Publishing Corp.

LIBRARY OF CONGRESS CATALOGING-IN-PUBLICATION DATA
NAMES: Chihaya, Sarah, author.
TITLE: Bibliophobia / Sarah Chihaya.
DESCRIPTION: First edition. | New York, NY: Random House, 2025.
IDENTIFIERS: LCCN 2024035563 (print) | LCCN 2024035564 (ebook) |
ISBN 9780593594728 (hardcover) | ISBN 9780593594735 (ebook)
SUBJECTS: LCSH: Chihaya, Sarah—Books and reading. | Chihaya, Sarah—
Mental health. | Critics—United States—Biography. | Books and
reading—Psychological aspects. | LCGFT: Autobiographies.
CLASSIFICATION: LCC PN75.C54 A3 2025 (print) | LCC PN75.C54 (ebook) |
DDC 801/.95092 [B]—dc23/eng/20240828
LC record available at https://lccn.loc.gov/2024035563
LC ebook record available at https://lccn.loc.gov/2024035564

Printed in the United States of America on acid-free paper

randomhousebooks.com

1st Printing

FIRST EDITION

Book design by Barbara M. Bachman

for the friends who brought me back

Oh, love is terrible, it is a *wrecker*—

—A. S. BYATT, *Possession*

CONTENTS

———

TEXTS

(IN ORDER OF APPEARANCE)

L. M. MONTGOMERY   *Anne of Green Gables; Anne's House of Dreams*

ROBERT MUSIL   *The Man Without Qualities*

GEORGE SCIALABBA   *How to Be Depressed*

ERI MURAOKA   *Anne's Cradle: The Life &*
(TRANS. CATHY   *Works of Hanako Muraoka,*
HIRANO)   *Japanese Translator of*
                                 "Anne of Green Gables"

HIROMI OCHI   "What Did She Read?:
                                 The Cultural Occupation of
                                 Post-war Japan and Trans-
                                 lated Girls' Literature,"
                                 Frontiers of Gender Studies,
                                 Number 5 (March 2006):
                                 359–63.

MARY HENLEY RUBIO   *Lucy Maud Montgomery:*
                                 The Gift of Wings

TONI MORRISON   *The Bluest Eye*

BJÖRK   *Post*

A. S. BYATT   *Possession*

MAGGIE NELSON   *Bluets*

JACQUES DERRIDA   *De la grammatologie*

ANNE CARSON   *Glass, Irony & God*

ERICH SEGAL   *Love Story*

RUTH OZEKI   *A Tale for the Time Being*

SIMON CRITCHLEY   *Notes on Suicide*

SARAH MANGUSO   *The Guardians:
                          An Elegy for a Friend*

HELEN DEWITT   *The Last Samurai*

DONALD ANTRIM   *One Friday in April*

UNKNOWN (TRANS.   *The I Ching*
RICHARD WILHELM
AND CARY F. BAYNES)

SIGRID NUNEZ   "The Art of Fiction no. 254"
                          The Paris Review

BIBLIOPHOBIA

Chapter 1

BIBLIOPHOBIA

It wasn't a surprise that I ended up in the hospital. The main surprise was how long it took me to get there. I'd been wondering about it for years, even fantasizing about it occasionally. It was just another little joke I had with myself. My breakdown would be both clearly inevitable (so nobody felt bad because it would obviously only be my fault) and gradual (so nobody would suspect there was a moment when they could have stopped it), but also would contain a sudden event (so everyone would know when it had definitively happened, which would be, no doubt, a relief for us all). It would have to happen while I had good health insurance, so nobody would be put out financially. My breakdown would be perfect and considerate. My breakdown would be so lovely you'd weep with delight. It was the project I'd been working on longest and most passionately; it was my masterpiece. When its time came, my breakdown's formal perfection would astound everyone. The reviews would be raves across the board.

The thing is, nothing really tells you when it's time to com-

mit to a nervous breakdown; it has to happen on its own
schedule. Once every few months since I was about ten, I'd
administered little check-ins, at first unconscious, then very
self-conscious, to see if it was time or not. These check-ins
were like the survey you get in an urgent-care waiting room, a
brusquely official interrogation I conducted to see if it was
finally time to start my breakdown, to just not get up one day,
not go to school or work, not speak, not continue. The survey
had gone through many iterations. In recent years, it looked
something like this:

Is it time for your breakdown when you sob frighteningly every day when you wake up (or go to sleep, or try
to have a nice lunch with an innocent friend who just
wanted to have a nice lunch, or get on the train in the
morning, or call a Lyft at 3:00 A.M., or turn on the
computer)? Probably not, because you're just crying, for
God's sake, and you cry all the time what with all the
current apocalypses, especially if you're not doing so
well at work, or you spent too much time reading com-
ments online, or people are moving on with their lives
around you, or families are making their normal, irremediable family trouble.

Is it time for your breakdown when all your just slightly
bad old habits start making cameo appearances, then
quickly insinuate themselves into indispensable side-
kick roles before you even know it? And suddenly,
you're a moderate smoker, a self-harm hobbyist, a casual insomniac, and a nonchalant bulimic, when you
used to just cycle through those things one or two at a

time? Definitely not. Surely if you had proper grown-up depression it would be more serious, like alcoholism or a sex addiction or a gambling addiction. Everything is fine because you only smoke four or five cigarettes a day and you're a miserly, mostly celibate hypochondriac whose credit rating is GOOD approaching VERY GOOD.

Is it time for your breakdown when the people who know you best, and a startling number of people you barely know at all, have asked you gingerly if you have a good therapist? Ha! This is a trick question.

Is it time for your breakdown when you've had writer's block for the last five years and when you sit down at the computer every day to accomplish your customary nothing, you hear the voice of your meanest ex in your head saying coldly, "It's like you're a depressed 1950s housewife who tells her husband that she's running errands but just goes out and rides the subway all day"? Remembering that voice makes you understand more and more that this particular ex always thought you really were crazy in a boring way, and not even that smart, and that he never bothered to hide it. Then you start to think he was right; after all, you *have* been lying to everyone this whole time about "writing a book," when all you've been doing, metaphorically but sometimes literally, is just riding the subway day after day after day. Thinking about this, you suddenly feel a tremendous guilt for lying to everyone about work, and a tremendous fear that they will all find out that you've been lying this whole time about being intelligent. Really, you're very stupid, and possibly insane. But come now, there's nothing actually wrong with you, you're just extremely lazy.

Is it time for your breakdown when every time a train approaches, or you peer out a high open window, or you stand in front of a busy intersection, you feel a wild fire-cracker explode in your chest, and the force of that explosion almost pushes you forward, and as you pull yourself back you have to hold in a bark of laughter you know will be rusty and inhuman? No, no, now you're just being histrionic. Nobody feels that, slash everybody feels that. It's fine, it's fine, it's fine, it's fine, it's fine. It's fine.

It was never the right time to announce my breakdown—to let everyone know that it was about to start. I wasn't even exactly sure what "nervous breakdown" meant these days anyway. It used to seem like a thing you could have in any number of dramatic ways, or at least that's what the novels and movies made it out to be. It could have been the DTs, or an office meltdown (say, throwing a typewriter or jumping out a window), or not picking the kids up from school one day, or a bottle of sleeping pills that you meant or didn't mean to take, or running away with the neighbor's spouse, or disappearing, or appearing too much. It could have meant a psychotic break, or a suicide attempt, or catatonia. Now, it seemed a little less clear, a little more nuanced. Doctors and Netflix warnings tell us to ask for help if we indulge in suicidal ideation or dark and violent thoughts or if we don't want to leave the house, like, ever. But surely, for me, those were not breakdown-worthy signs. I felt, indeed still feel, confident about these quotidian things. Leaving the house is overrated. Creativity is violent. Suicidal ideation is the lightest, easiest thing in the world. It's an invisible hobby, a fun little secret you can take anywhere, like doing Kegels at brunch or doodling in a lecture.

One thing I was pretty sure about "nervous breakdown" was that it was not for people like me. Nervous breakdown was not for the children of immigrants. It was something that happened to white people in independent films or in middlebrow realist novels. Breakdown was what happened when their gorgeous shells became so brittle and delicate they could be shattered with the slightest tap of the back of a spoon—tenderly set and ready to ooze out of their gelid whites with a hot, vividly compelling, golden violence. Breakdown was for Gena Rowlands in that Cassavetes film, magnetic in her housedress, all sharp knees and elbows and that rude, sexy slash of a mouth, that scrambled bouffant; breakdown was for the unseen businessman in the ominous Hawaii ad that Don Draper pitches in season six of *Mad Men* ("Hawaii: The Jumping Off Point"). I had had a lot of privileges in my life so far but breakdown was not one of them. Breakdown is the final frontier of assimilation. Of course, I didn't resent this. My breakdown was my personal hobby; it was not part of the job description for my parents' child. Quiet desperation or silent seething anger? Yes. Showy mental collapse? No. There was no time or money or feeling allotted for my breakdown, so if I really had to have it, I had to work hard and save for it myself.

Given all of this, I was certain that it would never be time. Other things happened while I pondered this problem over the years. I was depressed, I was not depressed, then I was depressed again. I attempted suicide three times between ten and eighteen, but to my eye those attempts did not look like good enough reasons to have my official breakdown, so I went on. I went to school, then more school, I got a job. So, why was this time different, after all those years? Why did my breakdown finally arrive?

*

At first, the unit seems like a textless place. It unfolds in a blank spectrum of neutrals, from the oatmeal floor tiles to the grayish ceiling tiles to the blond wood of the nurses' station to the inexpressive burgundy of the vinyl chairs we sit on to eat or color for mindfulness. This politely unemotional red usually appears in places that might benefit from its sedative effect, like the waiting room of the bank or the dentist—or here, in the inpatient psychiatric ward of a hospital, placidly enfolding stackable chairs. A few patients make oblong laps down and back on the featureless hall, feet in dull ochre standard-issue slipper socks that squeak softly on the polished floor, faded blue hospital pajamas flapping around bare legs. Very slow, almost inaudible. All the surfaces are smooth, except for our thin cotton blankets and thin cotton towels, which are coarse but clean and white. Neutral, neutral; everything safe and neutral.

But there are words here and there. The nurses' station is full of notes about us, about our medications and our frequently tested vitals and our participation or nonparticipation in activities and our medical histories, but those words are not for our eyes. The bulletin board opposite the nurses' station has text that *is* intended for us, written in neat, teacherly handwriting: the schedule of art or music or horticulture therapies, the list of lucky winners whose presence is "requested" at group therapy that day. The other text available is the menu, from which we choose our meals for the next day, should we care enough to choose. I usually do not; the small print is overwhelming and the words unappetizing, and it makes my head ache in a muffled way. There is also the television, rarely on. One day the president delivers his State of the Union address, but the words running in the chyron below make as little sense as the ones coming from his puckered lips.

There are a few magazines in the room I share with my sweet, fearful roommate, a woman on the cusp between extremely late middle age and elderliness named Rosemary, but I don't look beyond their covers. They are all cat-themed, and I'm not sure if they're hers, or if the hospital put them there for us, Feline Spinster Major and Feline Spinster Minor: a fanned-out selection of *Cat Fancy, Modern Cat, Inside Your Cat's Mind.* The last strikes me as insensitive to the occupants of the psych ward. What if one of us actually does think she is inside her cat's mind? I feel indignant, but also very seen.

My inclination is always to fall back on the easy humor of absurd set pieces like this, especially when things are not funny. I tried making jokes after a few days in the hospital, but they didn't fly with anyone except my assigned social worker, who would indulge me with the occasional tolerant smile. I tried and failed to lighten the mood during my friends' brief visits. "All the greats were in the loony bin," I declared with a perverse jollity that was half-fake and half-real. "I guess I'm a legit midcentury lady writer now."

But the hospital is not a funny place. It is still hard for me to admit that fully because it means admitting that the hospital is a serious place. I was there because I was ill, and the circumstances of that illness were not funny at all. I felt this unfunniness powerfully in the first couple of days I spent there in bed, lying under my rough white cotton blanket, curled to the rough white plaster wall—looking hard at nothing and feeling taxed by the sight of it, not yet allowed my own clothes or phone or other marks of selfhood and feeling like nothing. Yes, Rosemary was a sweet old cat lady, and I a harmless if not sweet youngish one, and it was all too easy to perform outrage at the sight of the cat magazines pointedly left on our side table. But Rosemary was also a lonely, debilitatingly anxious woman who needed saccharine, dishonest reassurance that she would get out soon. She needed to tell me how afraid she was of tomorrow's electroconvulsive therapy and wanted to know what I'd said or done to get out of having ECT myself; needed to talk in her thin, wavering voice to fill the nonconsensual intimacy of our double room. And I—well, I have no idea what I looked like or what Rosemary thought I wanted or needed, but it can't have been good. I did not want to talk. Those first few days I wanted to sleep, mostly, and when awake to look at nothing, to try and stop the whirring of mental processes and just lie very, very, very still.

*

Reader, it was the books that did it. They were everywhere. There was no space without them, no place in my home where I could rest my eyes or my brain. The overabundance of books had been a communal joke in graduate school. We all had more books than we needed and felt certain that we needed more still; we knew it wasn't true, but secretly still believed that the more books you had, the more serious you were. Those of us who didn't have secret family money took out more loans or degrading content-generating jobs for them. Everyone's apartments were bursting with books: books for seminar, books we were teaching, books for prospectuses or dissertation chapters, books that kept getting renewed and renewed from the library, interlibrary loan books in their prim paper cummerbunds, books you couldn't find anywhere and had to order from mysterious secondhand sellers on other continents, books borrowed from friends, books that showed up dog-eared from the used theory and criticism section at Moe's Books, sometimes so freshly resold and rebought that they had our own friends' or professors' names on their inside covers. Books, circulating and recirculating everywhere between us and among us like in-jokes or insults. Chains of volcanic book islands crossing floors. Books piled up, hoarderesque, in windowsills once the flimsy IKEA shelves were bowed with abjection. Books unread and gathering dust, growing resentful.

I am convinced that it is every writer's fear that our books will be the death of us. For me, for a long time, this fear was literal. I lived in Washington State and California for nearly a decade after college, but I never acclimatized to the West Coast, and my unserious but persistent concern about earthquakes condensed into an acute fear that my books would kill me. My time in the Bay Area was spent trying to disregard the cringing suspicion that my wobbly bookshelves would squash me flat with the slightest tremor; it turns out that being too lazy to anchor your bookshelves is the least sexy way to live dangerously. This, like many of my anxieties, is both literal and literary. While the fear of death-by-shelf is a very real, material concern, it is also an allusion to the death of the poor clerk Leonard Bast in E. M. Forster's *Howards End*, who ends up smashed under the symbolic weight of his earnest and unformed desire for knowledge, unfulfillable by dint of class and history—or unsymbolically stated, smashed under a large bookcase in a country house. I can't be sure what came to me first, the allusion or the fear itself. This happens a lot, that feeling when I can't remember if I thought a thought or if a book planted it in my brain, and it's just now popped up from wherever it was hiding. Part of my fate as a greedy, acquisitive reader is that I can never escape the overbearing presence of books, whether in the mind or on the shelf.

I wonder if, without them, I'd have any thoughts at all. Or if I would be anyone at all.

*

This used to be the very thing I loved about books. I loved that they were always there, and I loved the trust I had that there was a book for every need. But this love was complicated from the beginning. Reading was escapism of a kind, but not in the conventional sense. It was a way to get far away from my life, and to feel—not better, but simply *different*. Up until high school, I spent the hours between the end of school and the end of my mom's workday in our town's small public library. I roamed the shelves and picked books at random to read instead of doing homework, sprawled on the floor in the aisles. Even though the old library was tiny, and a surprisingly large part of it was devoted to the history of Hudson, Ohio, it still seemed curiously like infinity. All the feelings that anyone had ever felt, good or bad, seemed to be contained there, a thought that was more terrifyingly exciting—or excitingly terrifying—than comforting. I am disturbed and irritated whenever I encounter the moralizing claim that the main point of reading fiction is relentlessly positive self-improvement: Reading is good because it makes you good. To think of reading in this reductive way is insulting, both to books and to their readers. Being good, or becoming better—how can anyone think this is the limit of the literary imagination?

This way of thinking also presses the act of reading into a kind of service. Even pleasure reading is so often put to work in public discourse, producing politically expedient or personally therapeutic sentiments—the very worst writing about novels reduces them to factories for empathy and sympathy.* But why should reading always have to generate something useful, whether it be heartwarming inspiration or ideal liberal subjects? I want to think of reading not as productivity

---

* In *What We Talk About When We Talk About Books,* critic Leah Price describes various initiatives that connect reading to mental health and well-being, for everyone ranging from rescued cats and dogs to human patients of the UK's National Health Service. Linking these schemes up with other kinds of promises made about the various positive values of reading literature, she is troubled by the idea that books are literally prescribed as somehow curative:

> The NHS's claim that literature can heal lends institutional weight to what I'd long felt with more conviction than evidence: that texts *do* make something happen to their readers. What surprised and ultimately dismayed me, though, was the content of that "something." After years of turning to books for stimulus, I had a hard time accepting that they might settle or sedate. In overselling the book's power to calm and console, these therapeutic claims undersell its responsibility to upset and anger us.

but as a kind of *produce:* something that grows in whatever unpredictable way it will, sometimes smooth and beautiful and delicious, sometimes bitter and gnarled and thorny. I want to think with writers who, as Italo Calvino writes marvelously in *If on a Winter's Night a Traveler,* produce books as a pumpkin vine grows pumpkins; fruit for fruit's sake, not for the sake of whatever moral preserve or pedagogical jelly might be made of it. And I want to read as though eating whatever grows on those vines—an operation that is at once thoughtful and sensory, absorbing thought with one's whole body. Sometimes it is nutritious. Sometimes it is poisonous. Sometimes—surprisingly often—it is both.

For better or worse, you are what you eat. The books that refuse to be easily digested, the ones that churn up anxieties and fears you never knew you had: *These* are the ones that have most strongly shaped my own experience of reading as an adult. Looking back, they shaped even some of my earliest and clearest memories of reading—both books and the world outside them. I've only recently come to see that my relationship to books has become, or perhaps has always been, an uncomfortable but necessary vacillation between love and terror—between bibliophilia and bibliophobia.

*

There are two imaginary texts that have always been on my mind, stories that offer the comforting illusion of form in a formless life.

The first is a creation myth of sorts. Since I was a child, I have secretly believed that if I read enough, one day the right book would come along and save me. It is perhaps the closest

thing I've ever had to a religious faith. It's like the fanatical
conviction certain die-hard romantics have that one day
they'll just "meet their person" and life will truly begin.
Through all these years and all these thousands of books, I
have been looking for a text that would explain everything to
me (by which I arrogantly mean myself and the world and
how those two things relate) and, in explaining, make clear
the way out of the limbo I'd always been stuck in. I have au-
ditioned many books for this role over the years and no matter how many of them don't work out, I always believe that
the next one will be it. The last page of that book would be the
first page of my real life.

But like all creation myths, it is inextricable from a story of
destruction.

For many, many years, I had the queasy feeling that my life
was a book that was not very long and not terribly interesting.
I was never sure where I was in the plotline and often felt like
I'd lost my place. Whenever things got dark and muddled, a
singular way to resolve the narrative suddenly got very clear:
It could always just *end*. I'd find myself suddenly arrived at the
last few pages and eager to tear through them, even if just a
couple of days before it seemed that there were many long,
boring chapters left. It was a magical book; the table of contents could always shift, and the inevitable denouement could
appear at any time. To say it had a plot is perhaps inaccurate
because there was only one point that I was certain of, the
conclusion. I don't know where the idea of suicide came from
or when it came to me—it seemed inscribed in my pages from
the start, as though it were one of the unspoken rules of the
genre I was written in. Maybe it *was* the genre. It was never a
revelation, never a twist. I was always sure that the book of my

life would be a short one, and the last word had been set in type the day I was born.

These two stories needed each other. If I was, as I believed, headed inexorably toward this one ending, my only hope was to find the right book to wield before me and challenge my fate before I got there. This begins to make sense of why I was always reading with such vicious desperation, and maybe why the books that drew blood were also the ones that I kept closest. They were like talismans that, having taken something from me, might offer some protection in return. The books that frightened me, showed me the bloodiest and most essential truths, hurt me in a way I needed to be hurt, showed me glimpses of the real self within; I loved them more fiercely because of it. The moments when I'd felt the life-taking, life-giving power of books only made me ask more of them than I should have; books, like people, should not be asked to save us. It's not a fair demand. But perhaps some part of me also believed that I might need some darkness to fight darkness.*

---

* In her preface to the first edition of *This Bridge Called My Back,* a foundational anthology of writing by women of color—feminist critics, theorists, and activists—Cherríe Moraga quotes Audre Lorde on racism: "I urge each one of us to reach down into that deep place of knowledge inside herself and touch that terror and loathing of any difference that lives there." Thinking about this, Moraga realizes that that "deep place" is also where she must go in order to write, saying, "I know now that the major obstacle for me, personally, in completing this book has occurred when I stopped writing it for myself, when I looked away from my own source of knowledge." Place of knowledge, place of terror: Moraga goes on to confirm that these internal places are indeed the same. Knowledge and terror are embedded in the acts of both self-recognition and recognition of others, and it is those two things together that render us able to think deeply and clearly—and to write. To do so truly, we must, as Moraga exhorts, look determinedly into our deepest sources of knowledge and terror and draw what they contain up to the surface, onto the page.

I have come to understand that these myths are not myths at all. The book that would kill me and the book that might save me, sadness and reading, self-harm and writing, are the violent lifelong habits that made me who I am. For me, being a depressed person and being a reader-writer are knotted up in each other all the way back to the beginning. All my crises are scrawled in the margins of the novels I've read over and over again, sometimes to feel safe, sometimes to sink willfully into further despair. These are the books I want to reread here, to try and explain myself, knowing full well that explanation is impossible.

*

The waxed floors of the unit were shiny and quiet, except for the tiny whimpers of rubberized socks on vinyl. The large windows were completely soundproof, the Manhattan sky-scrapers sulking silently outside, dark gray against a pale gray sky. Some people talked during meals and some did not. After being a nontalker for the first couple of days, I took it upon myself to have one short conversation a day, to convince the nurses that I was trying, and would soon be ready to be discharged. I tried to smile in a neutral way, nei-ther unsettling nor inviting. There was never anything to say. Some people could not or would not talk. To ask too much about someone was unbearable; to pretend that we were having normal dinner chatter even more unbearable still. How did any of us get there? What were we doing, and when would we leave? The etiquette of the ward was differ-ent for everyone, and the rules were always shifting accord-ing to who came and who went. At any moment, any one

of us could trip and crack the stillness, fall through the
floor.

I did not share the circumstances of my arrival with any of
my fellow patients. It had happened very fast and very slowly
all at once, and I had no way of communicating that yet except in floods of tears and braying, coarse animal sounds that
didn't stop once they started. I certainly didn't want to unleash
those and put everyone off their tepid meals.

I did feel obliged to talk to my doctors—a sign, I supposed
wearily, that I wasn't completely broken after all. To my surprise, I looked forward to our brief once- or twice-daily meetings more and more as the days went by. I didn't want to
converse, exactly; I certainly didn't want to write, or to read or
think. I couldn't even keep track of the flustered excuse-
making professional emails I was sending desperately every
day and couldn't make sense of the answers when they came.
I didn't particularly want to listen, but I did want to interact
with words. I liked the directness of the doctors' questions,
which loosed in me an equivalent directness, freeing up strong,
sometimes ugly language that I wouldn't normally use. There
was an intense pleasure to it, not unlike the pleasure I used to
feel when writing endlessly in my diary as a teenager—the
thrill of language's recklessness. I talked because I felt, in a
clichéd but earnest way, that I had nothing to lose or, at least,
nothing that had not already been lost. I liked how they listened and nodded and made notes, and I liked that I had no
interest at all in seeing those notes. I did not organize the
words into argument or clever play or persuasion the way I
would in a conversation in my outside life. I just wanted to
roll around in these newly honest words. I wanted to steep in
them for a few minutes, and then not have any more words at

all until the doctors came the next time. Then, I could go back
out into the unit to traverse that long hallway on my squeaky
soles and not feel pressured by language for the rest of the day
and night.

I read only one book in the hospital: Tana French's *The Secret Place*. Becca had dropped it off for me the day I was admitted to the ward, after a long night under observation in
the ER, along with a plush rabbit and a brown paper grocery
bag packed full of Haribo gummies. It was not at all the kind
of book I usually read, which is why I think she must have
chosen it. For a couple afternoons, it gave me somewhere to
hide; I'd curl up in bed, facing the wall, clutching the rabbit,
gnawing on the gummies, tearing through this mystery novel
and trying not to think about where I was. I can't remember a
single thing about it now: not any of the characters, not the
nature of the murder or the identity of the murderer. It was
the last thing I read for many months.

*

BIBLIOPHOBIA: occasionally manifests as an acute, literal fear
of books, though more frequently develops as a generalized
anxiety about reading in patients who have previously experienced profound—perhaps *too* profound—attachments to
books and literature.* It can have many symptoms and can
appear as a diverse range of seemingly unrelated difficulties

---

* There is some clinical overlap here with *bibliolepsy*, as pathologized by
Gina Apostol in her study of the latter: "Bibliolepsy: a mawkishness derived
from habitual aloneness and congenital desire ... Biblioleptic attacks [are]
usually followed by bouts of complete distaste for words."

pertaining to books and reading. Bibliophobia can only occur when someone has, crudely stated, loved books to a dangerous degree. You may have bibliophobia if you frequently experience intense reactions to books that somehow act on you, or activate you, in ways that you suspect are unhealthy or hurtful—or at times, simply *bad for you*. And yet they are necessary; you would not be you without them.

Childhood symptoms of my bibliophobia included: violent fits of melancholy and resentment after finishing a book I didn't want to end. Superstitious fear of incompletion, lest the book know that I put it down halfway and be angry. Repetitive readings that verged on morbid obsession, or perhaps Caligari-like hypnosis. A devout belief in the totemic power of the individual book itself and a fixation on particular copies that could not be lost or replaced. This last actually continued embarrassingly into adulthood and translated into a peculiar horror of specific books that, for one reason or another, terrified me such that I had to hide or immediately dispose of them so they wouldn't somehow infest my living space— examples include Caryl Churchill's *The Skriker* or Sarah Waters's *The Little Stranger* (which I had to shamefacedly go and buy right back from the used bookstore in grad school when I decided I actually wanted to write about it).

Advanced symptoms of the adult bibliophobe: alternating rhapsodic delight and gripping anxiety in particularly good bookstores; fear masked as arrogant resistance to certain books I was meant to have read but was secretly sure I could never understand (I'm looking at you, *Ulysses*); creeping suspicion that I am not a person but a card catalog of the books that I've read. The notion that certain books—you never know which ones!—can somehow overpower or enthrall their readers, such that we might never escape them. But while the idea of living in a book appealed to me as a child, as an adult it seems more and more like plain old madness.

*

Bibliophobia is many things. It is about the fear of the *idea* of books themselves, of particular books I have known, and of a specific, unknown and unwritten book: my own.

At some point in my dramatic adolescence, I decided that I was allowed to die after I wrote one good book. Sometimes, paradoxically, I thought this one book could be everything: both the book that saved me (because surely it would make me eternally famous) and the one that killed me. This conviction, irrational though it is, has never left me. One book— I didn't even have to see it in print, the posthumously published work appeals to me—and I would be finished, free.

When my bibliophobia really started to build, leading up to the long-anticipated breakdown, I had been working fruitlessly on many different versions of the book I was required to write for my job as a tenure-track professor of literature: my first academic monograph. "Nothing good is *mono*," mused my friend Sophie, also a writer and disgruntled scholar. "Monograph, monotony, monogamy . . ." Of all the genres that populated my dangerously overstocked shelves, this is the one that terrified me the most: the standard, hoop-jumping, tenure-getting first book composed of a smart introduction, four pertly observant chapters, a pithy or provocative conclusion, a long bibliography. It seems so simple laid out like that. Part of my terror came from this perceived simplicity. But another part of it came from the long-held certainty that I only had one book in me. Was it really *this* one?

"Just write your book," my senior colleagues would tell me as we breezed by each other in the hallway. "Just write your book," my father sternly told me on our increasingly rare calls. "Just write your book," said my nonacademic friends, puzzled as to why I'd been working on some mysterious air-quotes "book project" for so many years with nothing to show for it. But more and more, every time I sat down to reread what I'd done, or even to hash out the most basic copyedits from finished sections, I slumped over, my body falling in upon itself. In the months leading up to my hospitalization, actual physical disintegration set in like a punishing plague, an event I now find hilariously literal-minded: Coming back from my first day of the fall semester in 2018, I developed a wide swath of oozing boils across my shoulders that were biblically revolting and mystifying even to a dermatologist.

Apparently, an intervention was called for. Sitting at my kitchen table one day that fall, my friend Merve told me that I just had to write a book, any book, and that I should just start by writing letters to her. With our friends Katherine and Juno, we had just finished a collectively authored epistolary manuscript, the only sustained project I'd been able to work on successfully for years. Maybe it would work this time, too? Generous as this offer was, she had a steely, zealous immigrant-parent glint in her eyes, and I had at once the distinct, future-oriented, absurd feeling that I was experiencing what her teenage children might someday feel when she gives them a serious talking-to, and a jarring, pained flashback to my own childhood, being disciplined at the kitchen table by my father. There's something about that primal scene: sitting in my family's suburban dinette under a pendant lamp that comically hints at the single bulb of a noir detective interrogation, between the hapless cop that is my mom and the unhinged cop that is my dad, sweating under the pressure. I'm not sure if Merve did it on purpose, but this setup is a trick that works on me every time.

On that day, we were supposed to go pick up something to eat, but I had started crying—there was never a reason why in those days—and I could not stop. My sudden crisis was keeping us from lunch, another throwback to those family kitchen confrontations, which seemed to always be keeping dinner on hold. I told her tearfully that I was an ungrateful idiot who didn't deserve the life I'd been given. That everything was over because I just couldn't write the goddamned straightforward book required of me, and that I could name fifty other smarter, better people who should have the tenure line that I occupied so cravenly. That I had stupidly and selfishly wasted all my too-abundant, unearned chances, and because of this, I had to be punished. I couldn't do this *one stupid thing,* the only thing that everyone seemed to think determined my worth, and it just proved what I had always known to be true, that I had nothing worth giving. I didn't say it, but the words escaped and hung between us silently anyway: If I couldn't write the book, I might as well kill myself.

She blanched and looked terrified for a split second, but by then she'd heard me say things like this over and over again. She'd responded with gentleness, or fear, or patience, or a firmly held hand, or a joke. I looked into her stern but pleading eyes and could not tell her the truth. I promised I would continue writing, and so continue living. But I knew that I could not do the former, and I didn't want to do the latter.

Sitting in my campus office that semester, my desk facing the long wall where all my critical books were shelved, I felt an occasional panic that grew more and more frequent. I would try to look at a book I'd read before, one I thought I understood and perhaps knew well and even loved—say, Sianne Ngai's *Ugly Feelings*—and, peering inside, just not be able to make the words line up. Am I going crazy? I wondered, or am I just tired and scared that my career, which is to say my life, is over before it has even begun? I became sickeningly afraid that I had lost myself, not in books that drew me in, but among books that shut me out. Looking at these books, I felt shunned, like I'd walked into a chamber full of hostile turned backs. I felt more and more certain that I had been pretending this whole time to understand a world that I fundamentally did not, and I had exhausted my resources trying to keep up the illusion.

It's understandable that nobody noticed that I was gradually losing my mind, because these are perfectly normal conditions for the untenured scholar. I was the luckiest of these—I had a job. The job is what kept me going, in both good and bad ways. It was, after all, another reason it was not time for my breakdown; there were students and colleagues relying on me. And, more pressingly, I had nothing to complain about, having miraculously made it out of the vicious academic job market employed and visibly unscathed. I tried not to worry about my worsening book fear. Everyone felt this way or worse, I told myself, and everyone *else* is dealing with it like adults. I did my best to hide the fact that I could barely bring myself to read more than a paragraph at a time, much less write anything, to varying degrees of success. I made it to the end of the semester, limping through the long, darkening fall months. But then winter came, and with it, the long-awaited collapse.

When I came back from the hospital in February, my bibliophobia became an acute physical condition: I would look at a series of words and just not be able to make sense of them. It wasn't just books. Internet hot takes made as little sense to me as critical theory, everything just blurring into shapes. My doctors guessed that it was due to a new medication or an emotional decompression period after my hospital stay. But I believed then, and still believe a little, that this new disaster—the consequence of having allowed myself a breakdown—was punitively moral. I had failed, as a reader and as a writer, and this was my fitting punishment. I had one task—one book to write—and I had not completed it. I had failed books, and I did not deserve them anymore.

At this point I became secretly, confidently certain of what ailed me, despite what the doctors thought or what diagnoses they offered. Bibliophobia, a concept I'd been kicking around as a premise for a darkly comic campus novel for years, became an umbrella term for everything that had gone wrong; it turned out that my own life *was* that unwritten absurd campus novel. I glared at the books that lined the walls of every room in my apartment; this was their fault! Or my own for not being able to deal with them. I learned another new word (a real one): "anhedonia," the inability to feel pleasure. In these months of not-reading, I felt nothing. Not only did I fail to enjoy anything, but I was also drained of the active despair of the before-breakdown months, and nothing had filled the empty basin of feeling it left. I could not make this new state of bathos funny, either, nor did I have the energy to try. I suspected that the reason I was not having feelings was because I was not reading books. This suspicion worked its way into my account of bibliophobia: If everything I am or have been has come from books, without them, I am a total blank.

The peculiar thing about bibliophobia, though, is that it tends to eventually produce more books. Sometimes those books end up being, if not a cure for their stricken writers, then at least an analgesic. This is an odd phenomenon. It seems obvious and natural that bibliophilia should lead to the production of more books. In *Loving Literature: A Cultural History*, scholar Deidre Shauna Lynch quotes the nineteenth-century editor and poet Leigh Hunt's delight at the idea that those who love books inevitably end up producing more books: "How pleasant it is to reflect, that all these lovers of books have themselves become books!" One might assume that the opposite would be true of bibliophobia. Why should the fear or anxiety bred by books be assuaged at all by the production of still more books, or worse, the transfiguration of oneself into a book?

This idea of becoming a book was particularly horrifying to me, and the idea of writing a book when I could not even start reading one was inconceivable. Yet eventually, it was the very idea of writing about the thing that prevented me from writing that offered the first hint of a way out of my torpor. A few months after the hospital, I recalled a line from a book I'd read some years ago, Geoff Dyer's *Out of Sheer Rage*. In it, Dyer announces his intention to write "a sober, academic study of D. H. Lawrence," and in so doing, "pull [him]self together." What follows is a comic, tragic, delightful, horrible account of his failure to do so. The line that returned to me is from the very end, after the various convolutions of travel, criticism, and relationship woes that a customary reader of Dyer's work might expect. In the end, in a moment of total, vulnerable exposure, Dyer realizes that "the more I ponder these questions the more I am persuaded that the real subject of this book, the one that writing it was an attempt to evade, is despair." Dyer's serious book about Lawrence turns out to be another book he had to write, a book about his own depression. It is this revelation that results in the continuation both of his life and his writing career and ultimately this not-always-serious book about D. H. Lawrence. He begins to read about depression, and then reads more and more, until he's writing a book about these readings:

> Nothing interested me—and this, in the end, is what saved me. I had no interest in anything, no curiosity. All I felt was: I am depressed, I am depressed. And then, this depression generated its own flicker of recovery. *I became interested in depression.* . . . I became interested in things again. I began to follow things up.

Depression is the hidden non-plot of the whole book, but Dyer can only admit it at the end. It explains everything and does not explain anything at the same time. When I recalled this moment, I still couldn't read, and so couldn't leaf through *Out of Sheer Rage* to look up its exact wording. But it made me wonder.

*

It took me a long time to get *interested* in depression the way Dyer was. The thing that seemed the most pressing to me, far more pressing than the state of my emotions, was the inability to read. I didn't exactly want to be reading, but I remember experiencing a muffled panic all the time, wondering what I would do if I could never read again. I had no other skills, I thought; reading is the only thing I'm good at. Since I was four, I'd never gone so long without reading every day. Without it, I had no escape from myself. This seemed worst of all.

Reading was my whole life, whether I liked it or not: My work life and my home life were built around reading, my physical space constructed by walls of books. All of them were useless to me now, and, looking at them, I felt nauseous. I lay in my apartment every day, allowing myself to be slowly upholstered in cat hair. I wondered vaguely if Rosemary was doing the same, wherever she lived, or if she was still in the hospital. My new medication made me foggy and slow; for the first time in my life, I became the kind of depressed person you see in the movies, sleeping fourteen hours a day and unable to stay upright. I might still be there if not for the brusque, Mary Poppins–like intervention of Merve, who, again, saw from afar what was happening and was having none of it. "Just come stay with us here," she insisted every day when we spoke. After a few months, I gave in. She had immediately dropped everything and flown to my aid when I was in the hospital; she stayed in my apartment with the cat and came to visit me on the ward every day, bringing an assortment of my least stressful friends. I was convinced that a change of scenery would do nothing for my condition, but figured I owed it to her, to show that I was trying.

"Here" was Oxford. I did something I'd never done before: tested my credit limit by putting a last-minute ticket from

New York to London on a card, found a friend to take care of the cat, and just ran away. I did not bring any books. We had made no plans about what I'd do when I got there, except, I supposed, be under constant supervision by Merve and Christian and their two small boys. They lived in a little hobbit house built into the wall of the college, which didn't afford enough privacy or space for any kind of suicidal shenanigans. Besides, the children! It turned out everyone was too busy to make plans for me, which was an incredible relief. At that moment, it was the most effective therapy just to be forced to participate in the everyday life of the household, to tag along after Merve to pick the kids up from school, to do the dishes, to run out for groceries when the other adults were occupied with childcare or emails. I made family meals and felt truly useful for the first time in several years. I felt simultaneously like the babysitter and the babysat.

During the day, there was nothing to do but go to work with Merve. She is the most disciplined writer I know and having a weepy lunatic to look after was not going to stop her from putting in a full day at the office. The first day felt like starting a new job: I didn't know what I should do, but I was too embarrassed to ask. Merve sat at the desk, whipped out her laptop, and briskly started typing away. She is a very aggressive typist. The low, rapid muttering of the keys made my skin crawl a little. I did not want to get out my computer because I couldn't think of anything to do on it, so I yawned dramatically and said I'd go pick us up some coffees. I took a long, slow walk past the Covered Market, passing several perfectly fine coffee shops on the way, then a long, slow walk back, returning with two tepid flat whites in hand. Merve's typing chattered on steadily as I slouched down into the tiny sofa, drinking my coffee and staring out the window. The sofa felt like it had been made to support the dainty tea-sippings of Regency aristocrats, not twenty-first-century invalids with poor posture, and I started to feel my muscles tightening in familiar, panicky ways. The typing got louder and louder. Eventually, I gave up.

I said: I can't remember what I'm supposed to do.

The typing stopped and she looked at me quizzically.

> **M:** Read something.
> **S:** I told you, I can't read anything.
> **M:** Maybe you can here.
> **S:** That's crazy. And I don't have any books.
> **M** (gesturing at the shelves): We are in a room made of books.
> **S:** I can't pick a book.
> **M:** Read DeWitt, I told you, you'll like it.

I probably looked like I was getting ready to sulk, because she got up and marched me down the winding stairs, down Beaumont Street and Magdalen Street and Broad Street, straight into Blackwell's, directly to the fiction section. There was one copy of Helen DeWitt's *The Last Samurai* on the shelf. We bought it and marched right back.

The typing resumed. I sat back on the tiny sofa. I looked out the window for a while longer, then looked down at the book. It was long. I opened it to a page at random and found myself facing what seemed like a series of Greekish words, or at least words that were Greek to me, screaming louder and louder at the top of their typographical lungs:

First "OKTOKAIENENEKONTASYLLABIC"
then "ENNEAKAIENENEKONTASYLLABIC"
then "HEKATONTASYLLABIC,"
whatever any of that meant.

I shut it instantly. This was the second thing that did not make me want to read the book. The first thing was its title: a book by an apparently white American writer called *The Last Samurai*. The queasy suspicion of orientalism was winding arabesques in my stomach, but there was nothing else to be done; Merve was hard at work again, and I had no more excuses. I opened the book once more, at the beginning this time, and started to slowly read.

And, to my surprise, I kept reading. Haltingly, then faster, then greedily, the way I hadn't read anything for months and months. Any summary of *The Last Samurai* is laughably insufficient, and I don't want to ruin it for you if you haven't read it. The barest narrative bones are these: It is the story of Sibylla, a brilliant comparatist and single mother uniquely unsuited to this world, raising her young son, Ludo, a multilingual polymath. Rather than raise him without a father, Sibylla offers him a wealth of male role models, in the form of Akira Kurosawa's 1954 film *Seven Samurai*. Perhaps all you really need to know about the story of Ludo and Sibylla can be obliquely summed up in two scenes from Kurosawa that shape Ludo's understanding of the world and the people in it.

First: The samurai Kambei agrees to gather a force of fighters to help a group of villagers fend off bandits. To find men of the right skill and integrity, he devises a test. He sits in the interior shadows of a room and asks one of the villagers to call in a passing samurai from the street. Meanwhile, Kambei tells his young disciple, Katsushiro, to hide inside the door with a stick and bring it down on the man as he enters. Seeing this, an onlooker is appalled at the seeming dishonesty of this trick. Just watch, Kambei tells him. A good samurai will parry the blow.

Second: Kambei and Katsushiro, joined now by the worthy samurai Gorobei, Shichiroji, and Heihachi, come upon two men fighting with bamboo swords. The first, the master swordsman Kyuzo, easily defeats the other man with one elegant stroke. The loser complains, and Kyuzo calmly says that if they'd been fighting with real swords, he would be dead. The loser demands a fight with real swords; the same thing happens. He dies.

Ludo mulls over these two lines, which seem at first like such simple statements of fact yet suggest such depths of self-knowledge: A good samurai will parry the blow. If we were fighting with real swords, you'd be dead. Both lines express a kind of unwavering trust and confidence—in what the speaker believes others will (or should) be capable of, and in what he knows himself to be capable of. As I think back and reread the novel for the first time since that spring, they are the lines that stay with me, too. Like Ludo, I want to hold on to the certainty of these phrases; I want to be as sure as Kambei or Kyuzo. Not just about myself—about anything at all.

I'll be honest with you: In that first reading, I couldn't say exactly what it was about DeWitt's novel that brought back my ability to read. I could produce any number of arguments about why the book worked on me, all of which are a little true, and all of which are also insufficient fictions. It could have been the way the philology-obsessed novel brought me back home to the field that raised me, comparative literature.

Or relatedly, the way it makes its readers work on language with Ludo: The Greek was largely lost on me, but I found myself practicing kana alongside him as he learned Japanese, and eventually was as jealous as Sibylla at his superior ability to absorb the language I've been half-heartedly pretending to learn my whole life. Learning any language, we are forced to learn again how to exist in that tongue, forced to relearn how to read. And this is something Ludo does with unguarded openness, to his mother's (and his reader's) envy. It could have been this book's unabashed recognition of the futility of so many book-writing enterprises.* Or perhaps it was the fact that *The Last Samurai* is ultimately a suicide novel: one in which a suicide is mercifully allowed to take place, but also one in which another suicide is, we hope, mercifully prevented. It was probably all these things together, but alone, none of them seem sufficient to explain how it was that this particular novel, read in this particular moment, brought me back to books, and back, at least partly, to myself.

Or maybe it was just that, by making me relearn reading, the book made me realize that until this total breakdown, I

---

* "There are people who think contraception is immoral because the object of copulation is procreation. In a similar way there are people who think the only reason to read a book is to write a book; people should call up books from the dust and the dark and write thousands of words to be sent down to the dust and the dark which can be called up so that other people can send further thousands of words to join them in the dust and the dark. Sometimes a book can be called from the dust and the dark to produce a book which can be bought in shops, and perhaps it is interesting, but the people who buy it and read it because it is interesting are not serious people, if they were serious they would not care about the interest they would be writing thousands of words to consign to the dust and the dark.

"There are people who think death a fate worse than boredom."

was a terrible reader. A clever terrible reader, sure, but a terrible reader nonetheless. I was always reading *for* something: first, for comfort, for pleasure, for validation, for comprehension; later, for symptoms, for ideas, for citation, for tenure. And always, secretly, for salvation. But it is only since my period of nonreading that I am learning how to really read closely and deeply, but without expectations, either of the books I encounter, or of myself. For years, opening a new book had felt more and more like a room I suspected to be full of punishing traps. I had been afraid even to step over the threshold of a book, because I didn't trust my own instincts; I was sure I would be found wanting. I was afraid I wouldn't pass the test. I still feel this, less often but with a fair frequency. I still don't always trust myself not to walk into the trap—that trap of my own intellectual failures but also my own surfeit of thoughts, which may come crashing down on my head as soon as I turn that first page.

But a good samurai will parry the blow.

Chapter 2

CANADIAN WORLD

I have very few memories of childhood, and the ones that remain do not fit together neatly. I remember certain moments in filmic detail from a wobbly first-person POV, like when movies show a dog's eye view, trundling around clueless and low to the ground. My first memory is of the moments before I fell headfirst down a steep, uncarpeted flight of stairs in our house outside of Montreal. I was sitting on the parquet floor of the landing at the top of the staircase with my back to the steps, galloping a My Little Pony—Sugarberry—back and forth along the floor, and a pleasingly sharp note of vinegar pierced the sweet, rich smells that drifted up from the kitchen.

At that moment, Sugarberry decided to take an especially daring leap, and when I swept her through the air, I felt the odd sensation of slow-motion suspension that precedes a fall, as I tilted backwards into empty space. I do have a faintly hilarious memory of seeing the balusters, steps, and ceiling cartwheel by, but I'm pretty sure I edited that into the movie at a later date. The next thing I remember is returning to preschool with a Band-Aid covering the surprisingly small fissure in my forehead. The classroom bully, who, at four, looked every bit as capable of unemotionally clubbing a defenseless beaver to death as her fur-trading colonial ancestors, taunted me in French and convinced everyone that if they took the bandage off, they'd confirm that my head was full of dry elbow macaroni. But I don't remember how I got from one moment to the next, or what happened after. My next fleeting memory is of arriving in the States a year or two later. It was a very hot summer day and my shoes sank into the melting tar on the driveway of our new old house in Shaker Heights, Ohio. I had never seen the ground ooze like this before and felt the thrill of scientific discovery. America was apparently composed of entirely different materials.

Perhaps it's better to say that I remember very few *events* of childhood, and the ones that remain are disjointed, often unrelated and highly specific. But I do have many sensory memories of how the matter of the world looked and felt and smelled. The tar sticking to the soles of my Keds, for instance—I can still see how thrillingly glossy it was if you cracked through its dull, dry skin, and how seams of that gloss bubbled up when you stepped on a soft spot. The stuff of that distant past is all heaped up in a big jumble in my mind's basement: hot tar, old wood floors, the rough pulp of paperbacks, dog hair, my own severed ponytail that used to be long enough to wrap snakelike around my neck, and fabric, reams and reams of fabric. The too-smooth hand of a Japanese polyester knit (white with a print of creepy, faceless mice wearing human clothes) that my grandmother had made into twee matching rompers for me and my mom. The lightweight gray and black rayon weave and broad red elastic belt of the dress that I wore to my elementary school graduation, a hand-me-down from my next-door neighbor; most of my favorite clothes came from her, and were my favorites because they were store-bought, not homemade. The cool, deep lushness of good black velvet that my grandmother had elegantly tailored, at my bizarre request, into a blazer for my tenth birthday. The slick bounce of brightly patterned Lycra that my mom made into figure-skating tights and skirts, far nicer than the pricey ones you could buy in the skate shop. It's incredibly simplistic, but the textures of my childhood are really just that—textures.

Textiles were important to us. My grandmother was a seamstress at a company that made fancy dresses, and her sewing room was filled with random lengths and remnants of satin and silk crêpe and delicate semi-sheer rayon she brought home from the factory. My mother's workroom in our house was more modest, but always contained a little stash of current or future projects; some window in the house always wanted new curtains, or some Halloween costume always had to be planned. Surrounded by cloth, folded, swirled, wrapped neatly in bolts, I felt safe. When I'm in a state of panic even now, I sometimes open the closet door and lean my face and body into the row of densely packed garments hanging there. I barely sew these days, but it makes me feel secure to know that I have yards of linen and lawn squirreled away on a high closet shelf and under the bed, waiting to be made into optimistic sundresses; it's my equivalent of bars of gold buried in the backyard. The best days of my childhood involved going to Jo-Ann Fabrics with my mother to browse the large binders of patterns. We'd run our fingers along bolts of material lined up neatly according to color, grain, and fiber, filling our lungs with the briskly circulated box-store air, unnaturally crisp and wonderfully inhuman, with clean top notes of new-ness and starch.

I wonder if this is why the first books I remember reading as a child—*really* reading and inhabiting—are Lucy Maud Montgomery's *Anne of Green Gables* series. They are textured texts, whose prose often slides into hues of purple in its avid observation of the trappings of Anne's world. Montgomery notes the material of Anne's life with the magpie eye of some-one who loves pretty things and is offended to the point of disgust by ugly ones, like the harsh yellow-gray wincey dress she arrives in from the orphanage, or the serviceable gray and snuff brown of the unbeautiful dresses Marilla makes to re-place it. Much adoring attention is paid to the lovely gar-ments that follow: the rich glow of the brown gloria, a silk blend, that Matthew buys for Anne's first dress with puffed sleeves; the delicate swath of light green stuff like an armful of springtime that Marilla brings her to make an evening gown; the frothy white muslin that seems to suit her best; or later, the creamy chiffon that her college friend Phil embroi-ders all over with rosebuds. I know there were other books that came first, but it's Montgomery's eight satisfyingly fat paperback volumes that seem like the beginning of my read-ing life and are still here next to me on the shelf, at what feels sometimes like the end.

*

As far as I can tell, the whole point of childhood is learning to read. People and events and social cues, sure—but really, books. (I say this with the arrogant certainty of a childless person.) When I was sliding into or crawling out of one of the dark, immobile states that fill many of my few childhood memories, the only thing I could do was stay in bed and read. It was a way to be awake but not present; it was also a way to be "doing something" in the eyes of my parents, while actually doing nothing. As soon as I could read independently, it's all I wanted to do. When I started, it was just to find out what happened next; as my parents liked to tell visiting friends and boyfriends, when I still needed them to read picture books aloud to me, I would tap the book imperiously and growl "SAY IT!" if they dared go too slow or take a pause for breath. In the first grade, I burned through lots and lots of the mass-market children's series that proliferated at the time: *Sweet Valley Twins, The Baby-Sitters Club, The Saddle Club, Sleepover Friends.* I don't remember the content of these early reads or what it felt like to read them; they went in one eye and out the other, but I didn't care. I was hooked. I had not yet learned that there are ways to read such that books stay with you—*in* you—forever. I was years away from the understanding that there are certain books that modify your chemical composition so palpably you fear you might no longer breathe air or drink water. And it becomes clear that something ever so slight but important in the way you read the world is altered forever. These are the books that make us grow up or sometimes realize that we have long since grown up.

Anne of Green Gables, and the seven sequels that followed it, were not those books. But they were different from the endless, anonymous chapter books I had been reading. I could spend an afternoon with Elizabeth and Jessica Wakefield in their split-level ranch house (whatever that was) in Sweet Valley, California (wherever that was), and leave them behind at dinnertime without a second thought. As soon as I started the *Anne* series, though, I settled into late-nineteenth-century life in the small Maritime province of Prince Edward Island, and, between the ages of about seven and ten, I never really left. I kept a toe on PEI's red soil for years, and even through college, when I came home for winter break and needed comfort reading to anesthetize myself in the insomniac hours, I'd turn to *Anne of the Island* or *Anne of Windy Poplars* (appropriately, the volumes about Anne's college and postcollege years). There was a newfound satisfaction to reading Montgomery's books that had to do with being in a world so replete, so populated and so perfectly contained. At the end of the first book, a contented Anne quotes Robert Browning as she looks to the future, murmuring, "God's in his heaven, all's right with the world." That phrase still pops into my head unprompted, and I still say those lines to myself experimentally, wondering how anyone could ever have believed them to be true.

Anne of Green Gables tells the story of Anne Shirley, a red-headed, hot-tempered orphan from Nova Scotia who's adopted by an elderly brother and sister, Matthew and Marilla Cuthbert, in rural Prince Edward Island. Anne's notorious temper is matched and surpassed only by her relentlessly— some might say annoyingly—open heart and spritely imagination. Despite the many scrapes Anne gets into, her good heart and quick mind endear her to the Cuthberts, and to the citizens of the fictional town of Avonlea, inspired by Montgomery's own hometown of Cavendish, PEI. It's an ugly duckling story, too; though originally dismissed as homely, skinny, and freckled, Anne, by *Anne of Avonlea,* grows into a sylphlike, subtle beauty, with clear gray eyes described in every possible iteration of "starry" and hair that darkens to a socially acceptable auburn. The third book, *Anne of the Island*, finds Anne—a brilliant student and would-be writer—breaking hearts and winning accolades as a coed at Redmond College. Through these first three books, Anne is accompanied by a cast of friends who, though never really her equals, are her dear companions. In childhood, she imagines worlds with her sworn "bosom friend" Diana (that sweet idiot!), dull, sensible Jane, and poor lovely Ruby, doomed to flirt herself right to death. At teacher's college and university, she meets her intellectual equals, most of whom are intriguing non-player characters: Priscilla, with whom I was fascinated because she eventually marries a missionary and moves to Japan, charming but largely absent Stella, and the charismatic, more fully realized Philippa.

Things were less interesting to me after Anne got engaged to her longtime friend and erstwhile rival Gilbert Blythe. *Anne of Windy Poplars* takes the model that many of Montgomery's Anne-adjacent short stories do, with Anne as a kind of facilitator to other stories of Island life. She recedes further and further from the center of attention in books five through eight (*Anne's House of Dreams*, *Anne of Ingleside*, *Rainbow Valley*, and *Rilla of Ingleside*), as she becomes a wife and mother to a brood of suitably interesting children. At the height of my Anne obsession, I mainly stuck to rereading the first three volumes. I didn't want Anne to grow up and grow old and leave behind her life of bosom friendships and books.

Yet Anne herself was not my "bosom friend," nor did I want her to be. She was not a character I identified with— nor, as my students would say, did I find her "relatable." Anne was strange and special, different from the other people in Avonlea or Glen St. Mary, the village she and Gilbert settle in, and it was very clear that this was a good thing. As a child, I was afraid of being called "strange" and did not like being "special," even when it was meant as a compliment. My homeliness was not just a matter of red hair and freckles, but a face that was simply incorrect in my elementary school, where everyone was understood as Black or white. I suspected even then that some readers viewed themselves as the good—or, let's just say it, *superior*—kind of strange and special, and therefore "akin to Anne," and that this might be the intended response to the books. I often wished I could feel this way about my particular unfitness, but I just couldn't ever get there.

Anne and I were also different kinds of readers. As a swoony preteen in the *Green Gables* days, she often imagined herself as "Lady Cordelia Fitzgerald," an alabaster-browed romantic heroine, swept up in tragical (comical to the reader) tales of forbidden love. I didn't go to books to be a heroine. I went to books because I wanted to be—nothing, nobody. I wanted nothing so much as to be a kind of sociable air, circulating invisibly in the room, necessary but never noticed. This is how I lived in Anne's Avonlea and, in fact, the whole reason that I retreated there. I liked how the books and their world existed so wholly without me. I liked being able to be in it without having to hide from its gaze. I was not accustomed to sitting comfortably in rooms full of people, and there was something so new and pleasant about being a secret but welcome observer in the busy world of the book.

To live like this in books is to live in friendly but distant relation to another world. Sewing patterns sometimes refer to the "right" and "wrong" sides of fabric—the side with the pattern or texture is right, and its unpleasing reverse is wrong. Reading in this way felt like the right side of the weave, the opposite face of the blank numbness that I felt much of the time. The kind of reader I wanted to be then was, like Flaubert's description of the author of fictions, "like God in the universe, present everywhere, visible nowhere." This is exactly how I wanted to feel in a book, minus the God part.

This desire to just be air circulating slowly through a setting has shaped my narrative tastes outside of books, too. One of the annoying things I tell friends, usually in some cranky way about some exciting movie or TV show they want me to watch, is that my brain doesn't move fast enough for action. I am, in general, not so interested in what happens, but rather how it happens and what happens all around the happening. It makes sense, then, that I often have trouble directly explaining the events that happen to me, a difficulty that apparently extends to the way I think, the way I write, every way that I am. In telling you this nonstory about childhood, I have found it impossible to just state the facts. I can't pinpoint almost any of what happened then in single events, both because I could never directly look at them in the first place, and because I can't see them directly in retrospect now. I can only tell you how the tissue of time around and between them felt.

As a reader, I am always diffusing into the world of fiction. As a writer, I cannot solidify into direct statements. As a person, I cannot solidify into someone who makes anything happen. In my most lost moments, I see myself disintegrating and drifting into everything and everyone else, floating unseen and dispersed through the world the way I wanted to float unseen through the worlds of books when I was young. I am very certain that, for better or worse, everyone else I know is real, but I sometimes feel like my particles are too dispersed to ever come back together again. I often feel semi-visible at best, like a cobweb you don't notice until you've walked through it. There's a scarier version of this, from Robert Musil's *The Man Without Qualities*, in which the mad murderer Moosbrugger has visions in which only straining, invisible elastic bands keep him from spreading horribly into other people and things—but I try not to worry about it. I may have my little problems, but at the very least I am certain that I'm not a criminally insane Viennese serial killer.

But maybe there's a simpler answer to why I feel this way. Maybe my diffuseness began not with reading but with the fact that, as a child, I was always crying. I still am. I am always just a sharp word or a loud noise away from that feeling of dissolution that starts simultaneously near the brain and the diaphragm—a fine splitting somewhere in the sinuses up top, and beneath, somewhere deep under the breastbone, a quiet, hollow pain. Think about the phrases we use to describe the lack of integrity brought on by weeping: you "dissolve into tears" or "break down crying." You can even cry various parts of yourself—your eyes, your heart—right out.

*

There is an obvious reason that the fabric store felt safe and why I felt like I could breathe more, talk more, smile more in its mazelike aisles. My father had no interest in it, and he never came on these errands—not once that I recall. The Jo-Ann Fabrics on Route 91 was the only dad-free zone. Everywhere else, home or abroad, contained either the tense possibility of his presence or the jittery temporariness of his absence. Even school was not safe. Since he worked from home and much of his job happened late at night, on the phone with Japan, throughout high school he would appear unexpectedly at track practice, lurking outside the fence on the far side of the field, kicking at the grass and yelling angry corrections every time I ran by. As he drove me home, I'd press my cheek against the cool glass of the passenger side window as he fumed and steamed about how I'd lazily been landing on my heels instead of the balls of my feet, or how the ten extra pounds that were always there no matter how many I lost were still slowing down my cadence.

What did it feel like the rest of the time, everywhere else? I still feel it involuntarily in my body now. My fingers, resting on the keyboard, are suddenly cold. A chill thread tugs upward through my spine, snagging and gathering nerves as it goes. There is a slight, irregular flutter somewhere deep inside my chest. The curved outer rims of my ears ache weirdly like someone is pulling up on them. I hate to say "walking on eggshells" but it's a cliché for a reason—that's what it feels like, all this strange upward pull in the service of lifting me off the ground, so my footfalls cannot be heard or even sensed as vibration. To be in a house and hear the sound of a garage door opening makes me hold my breath even now, no matter who might be pulling in. When I think back to how it felt to live in my parents' home, my body immediately reconfigures into this obedient and fearful marionette, a shivering network of suspended parts that timidly awaits instruction to come together as a body in movement.

If I try harder than I would like, I can remember other things—things you might call events, I guess. But even those have a textural quality, like I can only reconstruct a kind of mental diorama of certain frozen scenes in fine decorative detail. The black and orange bits of hijiki and carrot that flecked across the white dinette wall when my father flung a full plate at it, narrowly missing my mother's head; I don't think she even flinched, it happened so fast. The details of the wide, shallow dresser drawer—satiny wood veneer with a cherry finish and fiddly, cheap brass pulls barely big enough to fit a fingertip through—that he threw at me, years later; the raw, unfinished edge that just clipped my upper arm as it flew awkwardly past and drew a slender cat scratch of blood that blossomed under the skin into a cloudy bruise.

When I think about it now, it was like the things around my father demanded to be thrown, and he could not say no. I can even make this revised image endearing: All those sad, inanimate objects wanted desperately to fly, and my soft-hearted father could not help but give in to their whims. For years, I had versions of the more ridiculous events of my childhood that I often told as jokes, a genre that I refer to as "Chihaya Hijinks," some of which were oft-repeated bits of family mythology that my parents found funny, too. It was only in the last few years that I have realized, largely after being reprimanded gently by friends and therapists, that these might be stressful stories to other people. They're still funny to me, though, because they have to be.

At this point, after years of intermittent estrangement and his diagnosis with Alzheimer's, I don't want to blame my father anymore for what has gone wrong with me. It feels too easy—lazy, even. I realize from talking to friends from similar backgrounds that my childhood was unfortunately unremarkable. My dad was scary and always unpredictable, but so are lots of parents. And lots of them are so much worse; we lived in a nauseating atmosphere of possible violence or near violence or mild violence, but as far as I know, it hardly ever erupted into real physical danger, for me at least. By the time I was around, because I was the baby of the family and a girl, my dad had learned to shove instead of hit, and he mostly yelled and threw things. I went through a tempestuous period in my twenties when I also yelled and experimentally threw some small things, paperback books mostly. Since then, I have felt a frightening, sobering sympathy for him—at least when I remember to. I'm afraid that we are very alike. I will never have children.

The truth is, I don't know whose fault any of this is: my unhappiness, or my father's, or anyone else's in our undramatically, ordinarily cursed family. There's no point litigating it further. I cannot make claims for anyone else, and any that I make for myself have begun to seem dishonest, cowardly, narcissistic. The one person I want to ask for an explanation won't ever give it to me; he cannot now and could not or would not before (when I'm feeling uncharitable I say "would not" but I know "could not" to be the truth). It's hard to stay mad at my father when he has become someone else: someone weak and frightened, who can barely form words, much less raise his voice. I don't know how to be angry anymore at this vulnerable stranger. And if not anger, I don't know what to feel.

(I need to say that he also had moments of intense joyfulness that were just as unannounced and sudden as his rages; on rare occasions, he was possessed by a kind of uninhibited, ferocious sense of play that I don't think I inherited, of which I am now a little jealous. I'm positive that every therapist I've had has been more interested in him than me, though what his diagnosis would be, we'll never know. He did grow somewhat more pensive and intermittently gentle in later years, perhaps as dementia was starting to creep in, and when asked if he would ever consider mental health counseling, would just ruefully say, "Ah! It's too late for me now!")

It seems to me now like I was deeply affected by some kind of environmental disturbance more than by the individual characters in my family, like I grew up in a series of houses that were always about to slide off a cliff. But despite my parents' efforts to maintain at least a structural stability, the inevitable natural disaster was also coming from inside the house—and not just the house, but inside me. There's a type of childhood memory that I don't think can fully be explained by a general atmosphere of fear and tension. Or rather, I've been in enough therapy to know that it is inextricably entangled with those things, and I guess comes directly from them in some obvious way—but I am more and more certain that it must be more specific than just that. When I slip accidentally into one of these memories, I find myself in the twin bed I grew up with, under the covers, swaddled in a set of sheets (a cotton-poly blend, cream with dark pink rosebuds like Anne's favorite dress) that I loved so much that I insisted on using them until they were skin-soft and almost transparent. I know these are the sheets and that is the bed from touch, but I cannot see anything—my eyes are closed. Sometimes I can tell that it is night and sometimes day from the soft red light that bleeds in through shut eyelids. In these memories, nothing ever happens; I just lie there, on my side, knees balled up to my chest and nearly falling off the right edge of the mattress, the way I slept until after college, when I finally made a concerted effort to start sleeping in the middle of the bed like a human being in a movie, not a feral cat squishing itself into the corner of a cage.

I always instantly feel again what I know I was feeling then: the dull throb of headache that comes when tears have run dry. It feels like an inner absence, like everything I contain has spilled out. I know I have been crying for a long time, perhaps for a reason but probably not. It is more than the dull throb—it is a dull *dullness,* a drained immobility that I would not have had words to explain then, as a child of seven or eight, except to say "I'm tired." It's a feeling that has been with me on and off as long as I can remember and is with me too often still. For a long time, I believed that these sightless gaps and blanks in my life were simply the result of my own bad manufacture. They were caused by some kind of internal flaw that replicated itself over and over again until my whole body was riddled with fault lines, ready to crumble and blow away. My central flaw is a sadness that seems to come from nowhere and cannot be stopped from spreading and corrupting every-thing it touches; the faults spread out beyond me and reached deep into the foundations of every house I've lived in. It's a sadness that so often feels like it is mine and only mine. But I've come to see that it also belonged to my father, and per-haps to parts of his family that I won't ever know.

This is the inborn flaw that fractures out to destabilize ev-erything. My parents, like many immigrants of their genera-tion, did not believe in the concept of mental health; everyone was either fine, or just complaining, or in my dad's words, genuinely "a lunatic." I am still secretly worried that I fall under the latter category, and that he did, too. I didn't receive an official diagnosis of major depressive disorder until I'd been hospitalized, after decades of what, in retrospect, were obviously serious episodes. For most of my life, I'd thought of our family flaw as an almost romantic melancholia or as pa-

thetic, self-indulgent sadness or even as straightforward, unavoidable madness. ("You're smart because of your mother,"
my dad said to me one of the last, rare times we really talked,
"but you're crazy because of me.") I wish that I'd had access
when I was younger to a book like George Scialabba's *How to
Be Depressed,* which gives a mercifully matter-of-fact explanation of what depression is, one that I would have recognized
immediately as my own experience and found helpful, perhaps even as a child: "We are all issued neurological shock
absorbers, usually good for a lifetime of emotional wear and
tear. But if you're equipped with flimsy ones, or travel an especially rough road, the ride becomes very uncomfortable."
Flimsier-than-average shock absorbers seems like a kinder,
clearer metaphor than the image of latent and irremediable
structural damage that I grew up believing in. I wonder if my
desire to dissolve into a text came from the feeling that I was
already fated to undergo a process of erosion and destruction;
I might as well get to the point of total disintegration as soon
as possible.

*

For all her starry-eyed ethereality Anne is very solid, very real.
We know this because things are always happening to her,
and she is always making things happen for other people. The
pleasure of the early books is that even the most ridiculous
anecdotal happenings take on the mock seriousness of a major
to-do, and Avonlea village life is full of pleasantly eventful
nothing. What's more, Anne always learns from the events
that happen to her—whether a lesson about vanity from ac-

cidentally dyeing her hair green, or a lesson about impulsivity from selling a cow that doesn't belong to her—and through them comes to understand exactly who she is, where she belongs, who she belongs to. Even the titles of the books announce this: Anne is always *of* somewhere. After an early childhood of belonging nowhere and to nobody, the firmness of her belonging is never again questioned.

This is another reason I didn't feel like Anne. I never felt, and in fact still do not feel, like I am from anywhere. My family did not belong in northeastern Ohio—less because people didn't want us there (though that was occasionally made rudely clear), and more because my parents were very certain that we didn't belong there. There were certain things we just didn't do that were scornfully labeled "American": go to Disneyland, for example, or exceed a certain body mass index, or pronounce words such as "tomorrow" or "sorry" with the flat nasal vowels with which our neighbors were tragically cursed. Though we left Canada when I was four, I was raised to believe myself fundamentally different from everyone I grew up with in the States; when we became naturalized American citizens when I was in high school, I felt upsettingly like I was even more permanently alienated from the person I was supposed to be. The rest of my mother's family was still in Toronto, where she'd grown up, and I had a preadolescent fantasy that there was a version of myself that lived there with them. When we visited in summers and holidays, the two of us would be stitched back together like Peter Pan and his shadow, but the rest of the time, I was only half of a self.

There was, in fact, an actual shadow half that I didn't know how to integrate. It was easy to feel Japanese Canadian, and

to get along with my aunts and cousins there, who looked and
sounded like me and were always excited to welcome us home;
the most exotic of them was from British Columbia. My father's family, however, was *Japanese*-Japanese, split between
Tokyo and the family home in the southern city of Kagoshima.
After my father, the oldest son, left for America, he was estranged from the rest of his family for more than thirty years,
into my early adolescence. We did not make a trip to Japan
until I was fifteen and my grandfather had passed away. During my childhood, occasional presents were exchanged by air-
mail, but as far as I was concerned, they emanated from a
vague idea of "Japan," which was exciting but also scary and
mysterious and had no direct relation to my life in Ohio. In
the years of my Anne obsession, I clung to the knowable idea
of being Canadian, while being Japanese felt frightening and
impossible. How could I be from a family that did not seem
to want to know me, from a place I could only imagine from
the contents of a once-yearly Christmas package? One of
those packages, when I was nine or ten, contained a scratchy
wool Japanese schoolgirl's uniform. It was densely woven and
hot, and I haughtily thought its sailor collar and scarf were
stupid and babyish. My dad made me wear it to school for
class photos, and I sulked all day. When the pictures came
back, I didn't recognize myself in them. But under the anxiety
and resentment, I felt something weaker than longing but
stronger than idle curiosity about Japan. What kind of girl
would I have been if I wore that uniform every day and only
went to school with other girls in the same uniform, with the
same black ponytail and fringe, and faces that made mine
comprehensible?

Because of the specific coordinates of my background, I was doubly fated to meet Anne Shirley. If I'd had an American family, I wonder if I would have been obsessed with the March sisters, dissolving into their lives in transcendentalist Concord instead; as it was, when I eventually read *Little Women* in fifth grade, I was scandalized and embarrassed at how much better I thought it was than Montgomery's series. But in elementary school, it was all Anne, all the time. When I wasn't rereading the books, I was wearing out our two-cassette VHS copy of the 1985 TV miniseries starring Megan Follows, long before *Anne with an E* was a fleck of dark back-storied grit in the CBC's eye. Knowing that I liked to read, my grandmothers in Toronto and in Kagoshima started mailing me Anne paraphernalia before I even started reading the books. It was like a literary arranged marriage—it was simply assumed that I would love Montgomery's books. This was not just an Obaachan mind-meld; Anne was a major celebrity in Japan as well as her native Canada. While Montgomery wrote other novels about other idealistic, imaginative young women—notably the far more troubling and autobiographical *Emily of New Moon* trilogy—Anne remained her most famous creation and made the tiny province of PEI a tourist destination.

Many of those contemporary tourists come from Japan, where *Anne of Green Gables,* known as *Akage no Anne* (Redheaded Anne), was first published in 1952, translated by Hanako Muraoka. As Muraoka's granddaughter, Eri, writes in her biography, the translation appeared at the perfect time, "when the country was just beginning to rise and people's lifestyles were becoming Westernized. Anne ... was the perfect democratic heroine for this new age." According to historian Hiromi Ochi, Muraoka's translations of the *Anne* series were part of an effort at spreading American values, encouraged by the Supreme Commander for the Allied Powers Translation Program and the Civil Information and Education Section. The CIE's explicit directive was to culturally reeducate the Japanese population in the ways of Western democracy; as such, "the general principle of selection of their library was intended to represent the US and its democracy and way of life" and ultimately "to soften the predominantly negative image of the US and promote the re-education program." Later, Anne's popularity in Japan grew to an even more massive scale following the release of a 1979 anime series, directed by Isao Takahata with work by Hayao Miyazaki, who would soon become the co-founders of Studio Ghibli.

While the CIE may have lumped Anne under the general category of American democratic heroine, Muraoka herself made it very clear that Anne's Canadianness was an essential part of her nature; as she wrote in her afterword to the first edition, "Although the country of Canada extends north from the United States of America, the Canadian people have a cheerfulness and simplicity that sets them apart from the Americans or the British." This benign fetishization of Canada has persisted, not only in the thousands of Japanese tourists who visit PEI every year, but in physical form in the center of Hokkaido, a couple of hours from Sapporo. There, outside the town of Ashibetsu, you can walk through the remains of a failed theme park called "Canadian World," a replica of Avonlea thousands of miles from the Maritime Provinces. Between its opening in 1993 and closure during the Asian economic crisis of 1997, Canadian World attracted thousands of visitors and hired genuine Canadian actors to move there and play the roles of Anne, Diana, and the rest of the cast. After it went bankrupt, the theme park became a municipal park; abandoned by its theatrical inhabitants, it's now a kind of Victorian ghost town in the middle of Japan's northernmost island.

A promo video from 1996 makes the then-flailing theme park look like a sunny, demure hell. Shots linger for far too long on an Anne lookalike awkwardly smiling and waving at costumed passersby from her perch on a split rail fence and on a young man who performs an increasingly dangerous act that begins with tossing his hat in a nifty way and escalates to fire juggling on a unicycle. Archery—not a significant Avonlea pastime, as I recall—is briefly advertised.

But the video that I keep going back to is entirely unpeopled. It's from a yet-unreleased documentary about the Japanese fascination with Montgomery's work. In the video, an unseen cameraperson walks slowly through the deserted park on what seems to be a hot summer day. The sound is purely diegetic: crickets and cicadas singing from the tall grasses that sway on either side of the red paved paths designed to look like the iron-rich soil of PEI; the footfalls of our silent guide; the tinny music piped in through speakers hidden throughout the park. The video culminates in a tour of a replica of the actual Green Gables house, accompanied intermittently by snatches of "White Way of Delight," what I can only assume is an Anne-inspired pop song with an irritating Christmassy vibe that plays in certain rooms of the house. The handheld camera has a *Blair Witch* quality that, combined with the empty house and desolate village, fills me with something like exciting, slightly carsick melancholy. The only thing that mars the effect is a red sedan parked on the side of a road, its trunk open but nobody around. It's an A24 folk horror movie I wouldn't mind being in.

*

There was one thing I did share with Anne, a trait that she herself had received from her creator, Maud Montgomery. Especially in the first three books, she is an unstoppable writer, from the fantastical romances she dreams up as a child, to the slightly less fantastical ones she sends to magazines in later years. It may in fact have been Anne's need to write that gave me the idea that I might also want to, or perhaps have to. But I had, and still have, an inability to determine when something really counts as an event worth recounting.

Montgomery seems always to have had a keen sense of what was worth writing down. From the age of nine she consistently kept a diary, a practice she maintained until her last years. Her official journals shed a fascinating light on what life was like for a female working writer at the time, balancing her demanding public life with her husband and children, and the duties of being a minister's wife. But in editing Montgomery's official journals and later writing her biography, Mary Henley Rubio found traces of a ragged, competing narrative of her life, especially the tragic, intermittently documented years at its end. Rubio highlights the gaps between Montgomery's three bodies of work: the sentimental, optimistic stories she published for the world to read; the multivolume journal she was assiduously revising for publication; and the other pieces of writing that she did not want to see the light of day—the ones that sketch out an incomplete record of her depression and despair, brought on by her husband's lifelong, debilitating mental illness, the many betrayals of her ne'er-do-well older son, and the psychic weight of living through two world wars.

A CBC news article from 2008, in which her granddaughter revealed that the family believed that Montgomery died by suicide, is what got me interested in finally learning more about her, after decades of being so close to her fiction. Rubio's biography, *Lucy Maud Montgomery: The Gift of Wings*, contains excerpts from Montgomery's last writings, which seem to corroborate this claim. On March 23, 1942, she wrote the final entry in the tenth and last extant volume of her journals, admitting that "my life has been hell, hell, hell. My mind is gone—everything in the world I lived for has gone—the world has gone mad. I shall be driven to end my life. Oh God, forgive me. Nobody dreams what my awful position is." A month later, just two days before the barbiturate overdose that killed her, she wrote a note stating that this last volume of her journals must not be published, for "parts of it are too terrible and would hurt people. I have lost my mind by spells and I do not dare to think what I may do in those spells. May God forgive me and I hope everyone else will forgive me even if they cannot understand. . . . What an end to a life in which I tried always to do my best in spite of many mistakes."

*

I've been lying to you. I've been avoiding the fact that there *are* events from my childhood that I remember as events, clearly and factually. Not because I think they're bad things to talk about, but because I am worried that in telling them, they'll be revealed as nonevents, and then where would I be? After all, is a failed suicide attempt an event, or the opposite of one?

The first time, I was ten and we were in our second house in Ohio—the first place we moved deep into whitest suburbia, forty minutes from my dad's office in downtown Cleveland. I had suddenly and inexplicably become very bad at math. I'd failed a test and brought it home over the weekend for my parents to sign. I must have been scared, but I only remember feeling exhausted. Rather than face this, I decided immediately that the only thing to do was kill myself.

I don't know what could have inspired this choice; I don't even think I knew what suicide was, really. I might not even have known the word then. Only now does it frighten me that this was such an obvious and easy step, even at that age. I was not distraught about it. There was something in me even then that did not worry about death, perhaps the same part of me that still sometimes smokes and doesn't ever wonder about what it would feel like to be old one day. Is this an inborn quality? To not fear death? Is it part of my Chihaya flaw? I remember once, when I was seventeen, my friend Tolu and I made a bad last-minute calculation in sprinting across a busy road and almost got hit by a car. We were so close I was sure I could feel heat coming off the silver body of the car as it sped past us, horn blaring. We hurled ourselves, panting, onto the pavement at the curb. Tolu was in a panic, tears streaming down her face, shocked at how close we had been to death, but I was laughing wildly. She stared at me. I remember the heat of her quick anger like the heat of the car, and I remember knowing that she was right—it was not funny, it should not have made me feel the strange burst of euphoria that I'd felt leaping away. She was right, but still, I could not stop laughing.

One of my prized possessions in that suburban house was an old commemorative issue of *Life* that featured tales from the Golden Age of Hollywood, including a short, sensational story about the life and death of Marilyn Monroe. From it, I learned that she had died of an overdose of "pills." I did not know what kind of pills you could die from, but the only ones available in my parents' orderly bathroom—other than the bottle of Seirogan, the vile-smelling stomach remedy that's ubiquitous in every Japanese home—were Tylenol gelcaps. The bottle was not half-full, but that seemed like enough, to a child who had never taken more than one at a time. I gobbled them all down as soon as I got home from school on Friday, and went about my business as usual, running downstairs to watch *Tiny Toons* and *Animaniacs* before my parents got home from work.

I don't remember how long it took me to start throwing up. I think I was already hanging off the toilet by the time my mom got home an hour later. I don't remember her helping me up and getting me out of school clothes, into pajamas, and into bed, but I do have a vague recollection of lying there, clutching a large red melamine bowl in case of emergency. I remember a sensation of clamminess everywhere, the chill of the air on my face. I remember an unfamiliar pain torquing my stomach, wringing it like a dirty sponge, and a strange, tangy bitterness on my tongue.

From there on, I remember it in the way I remember all the other moments lying in bed, weighed down by the dullness; dark but for the dim glow of the hallway light through closed eyelids, feeling something that was not a clear feeling at all, but its vague absence. What makes this memory special and different is that I clearly remember a sense of relief, even as my stomach scraped away at itself and my head felt oddly like it was both expanding and contracting. I felt a strange stillness, like the heaviness would keep me there in bed forever and keep everything quiet and easy and safe.

There are two more events—nonevents?—like this from my childhood. I might as well just own up to them now, so they can all be judged together. Attempt number two: wristcutting, aged fourteen (they were cowardly, shallow horizontal cuts; I didn't know any better, and didn't know yet that you could use the internet to learn about this kind of thing). Attempt number three: prescription medication, aged sixteen or seventeen. This last one was more serious, but not serious enough that my dad would let my mom take me to the doctor, terrified that an incident like this would go on some kind of panoptic permanent record and ruin my chances of getting into college. I remember being in an underwater state, listening to the spiky rise and fall of their panicked voices and not understanding them. The details might seem important, but they're not. All you really need to know is that, obviously, these attempts didn't work. And as far as I am concerned, the jury is still out: These episodes may or may not qualify as real.

*

One of the most jarringly realistic and tragic events of Anne's life has a dreamlike unreality about it. In the middle of *Anne's House of Dreams,* otherwise an insipid and fantastical romance tale, Anne is pregnant with her first child. But Joy, the baby that Anne delivers in June, lives only a few hours. For three pages, the house of dreams is filled with a terrible sadness, albeit one kept from getting too dark by Montgomery's customary amiable tone. True despair rings out for a moment as Anne questions how God could have let this happen:

> "It was God's will, Anne," said Marilla, helpless before the riddle of the universe—the *why* of undeserved pain. "And little Joy is better off."
>
> "I can't believe *that*," cried Anne bitterly. Then, seeing that Marilla looked shocked, she added passionately, "Why should she be born at all—why should anyone be born at all—if she's better off dead?"

Yet by the next page, Anne is already on the path to recovery; the episode is tightly contained. As a child, I disliked *House of Dreams* and did not frequently return to it, but every time I did, I found that I had forgotten about the death of the infant, which felt at the time like a strange, sad interlude. Rereading it now, I'm shocked at the smallness of this event in the scope of the book, especially considering that Montgomery considered her work literature for an adult audience. There's a sentimental dishonesty about it that upsets me, and I wonder how, as a younger reader, I was able to drift harmlessly through this episode with the same airy unconcern I applied to the rest of the books.

I've worried recently that there's something dishonest about the way I've learned, as an adult, to tidily fabricate stories about myself—stories that are also often falsely contained and impenetrably woven. Outside of them, though, I'm afraid that I am still as diffuse and unreal as I've always been, floating immaterially among the narrative events that I have carefully selected to make sense of my own nonsensical life, just as I used to float invisibly along the red dirt roads of Avonlea. But maybe that's true of all writers. Maybe it's true of all people.

*

I had desperately wanted to go to PEI to see the real Green Gables in the peak years of my Anne fandom, but it was not a possibility. The Maritimes were a zone of mystery in our house. Rumor had it that my parents, following a whirlwind six-month courtship and engagement, had embarked on a two-week honeymoon camping trip through New Brunswick, Nova Scotia, and PEI. There is little photographic evidence of this alleged trip, and I find it incredibly difficult to imagine my Torontonian parents, clad in tiny seventies shorts and white sun hats, sleeping in a tent along the Atlantic coast, hopping from village to village, going up lighthouse after lighthouse. They themselves rarely spoke of it. There was never any question that anyone in my family would ever return to the Maritime Provinces. I've sometimes wondered what happened on that honeymoon that made a whole region of the country inaccessible—perhaps they had committed some terrible crime by accident, and we could never go lest the fisherman they thought they had murdered was still haunting a stretch of beach by the Bay of Fundy or the Reversing Falls. Or, more horrifyingly, perhaps a chilling realization came upon them, after a very hasty engagement and marriage: that they didn't know each other at all and had fundamental differences that would make the coming decades more and more miserable.

It was only very recently, in rereading the Anne books, that it occurred to me that I am an adult, conceivably capable of visiting the Maritime Provinces on my own. And yet even considering it, I was flattened by a feeling of incomprehension and intractable difficulty. I did spend a few days investigating the best way to get first from New York to PEI, then from Charlottetown to Cavendish, where to stay, how to get around without a car. I clicked through page after page of accommodations with names like "Kindred Spirits Inn" and "Anne Shirley Motel and Cottages." I found myself staring at plane tickets and hotel reservations and discovered—unsurprisingly—that there is even a hotel co-owned and operated by a Japanese woman that appears to cater to Japanese tourists. I thought about what I would be doing there if I actually went. If I were writing a different kind of essay—say, a deeply researched long-form piece for *The New Yorker* or *The New York Times Magazine* on the relationship between *Anne* and Japan—I would have had to go. I would travel there without a qualm, I imagined, having made contacts to talk to and hoping to find Japanese tourists willing to put up with my vague sense of cultural comradeship. Thinking about it that way, the trip seemed doable, reasonable even.

But I couldn't click the button to buy the flights or book the hotels. All of a sudden it felt impossibly indulgent and irresponsible to go on such a trip. I imagined finding myself at the Green Gables homestead or wandering the carefully cultivated roads of Avonlea Village, among enthusiastically vacationing families and Japanese tour groups—always two of my greatest social fears. I'd just be a strange, solitary adult woman trying to connect with—what? What would I expect to see there? What would I want to see or find? I had this irrational feeling that if I even attempted to make this trip, the whole island would get swallowed up by the Gulf of Saint Lawrence and I would be held personally responsible to the nation of Canada for the loss of an entire province (albeit the smallest one). I immediately closed all the windows. The Maritime Provinces were not for me.

I can only speculate that it seemed fundamentally wrong to go physically to the places I spent so much time inhabiting spectrally. If I were to go to the Island, even to the contemporary touristy version of Anne's Avonlea, it feels like something would shift in the composition of my world; all the things that seem like nonevents would either be weighted with reality (and therefore consequence) or would dissolve into air (and become inconsequential). I don't know which of these possibilities is worse. It is safer not to try.

Instead, I keep watching the Canadian World video. I put it on a loop in the background of my desktop, so a part of the park is always slowly being revealed in the corner of my eye. Following the invisible presence of the cameraman through the deserted village, I feel strangely at home. Maybe this is the place for me, where I can be exactly what I hoped and feared I would become as a young reader: a ghost in a ghostly place, doing nothing, touching no one, diffused on the breeze like pollen spreading over the Avonlea fields.

Chapter 3

CUT, SHUFFLE, CUT

When I was an uncomfortable preteen, with a body I did my best to escape and a face I just couldn't wrap my head around, I devised an exercise that was halfway between a writing prompt and a kind of divination. I made a little deck of cards with different traits—eye color, hair color, names, and, because I was one of those children who is scared of people, charismatic animal companions. I read a lot of mass-market fantasy novels that made the rules of this game very clear: There were certain ways to look, certain necessary adjectives, certain clues as to what constituted a heroine. The ritual was always the same. Every day, I'd shuffle this deck, pull out a card for each feature, and line them up next to one another like a tarot spread. I'd ponder what the cards offered and conjure up a brand-new character. I'd imagine a detailed backstory and then draw a portrait of her in the sketchbook I kept hidden in my desk drawer. My characters were generally orphans: sometimes urchins with secret lineages or ladies who wanted to be rogues or spellcasters, the usual paperback fantasy stuff.

I filled the whole book with these rap sheets, sketchy premises for highly derivative novels I'd never write. My characters were always involved in adventure plots that skated on the edge of romance, accompanied by valiant, silver-maned steeds and talking ravens or hounds, but I was just in it for the simple act of imagining a new person into being. Naturally, my creations were all extremely beautiful, even if (or especially if) it took a discerning admirer to see it. The options dictated by the cards were things like amber, opal, or violet eyes, and hair like autumn leaves, or sunlight through honey, or the velvety night sky. They all had delicate faces and quick wits and low, mellifluous voices, and they darted through the worlds I imagined for them on lithe, nimble limbs. I didn't need to draw a card for the color of their skin or the cast of their features. They were always white. I did not imagine myself as them; I could not have. They were not me, but they were *mine*.

I can't remember most of the books that shaped this pattern of escapism. They were anonymous fantasy novels of the kind that proliferated endlessly in the eighties and nineties. I can't recall a lot of books that I read in the post-*Anne* era of later childhood. I wish I could, so I could go back to them now. I know certain special books almost by heart from repeated readings—ones by Meredith Ann Pierce, Madeleine L'Engle, Susan Cooper—but it's mostly a blur.

It's strange to think that I was always reading, but I can't say what I was reading. Once a week, I'd leave the library with an arm-length stack of Mylar-covered hardbacks from

the "New Books" section. I was so excited that I'd read the
first page of each one on the ride home, just to try and decide where to begin. I remember reading books pilfered
from my mom's library stack that terrified me or stirred up
unidentifiable feelings—at the time, she had a taste for spicy
historical fiction and medical thrillers—but her books also
offered uncomplicated and unmemorable pleasures. It wasn't
the books themselves that did anything; it was the feeling of
immersion. I wanted to stay inside that feeling, but I already
knew it was frustratingly temporary—no matter how hard I
tried to stay with them, books would always have their own
worlds, from which I was ultimately barred. This was a confusing and hurtful knowledge. I felt like I was the only person in the world who really *loved* books, and wondered if
books, in a strange way, could ever really love me back. That
desire to be loved back: That, surely, is where the trouble
began.

I do remember this kind of childhood reading seeming
safe and certain, but that safety was limited—sitting alone in
my room, library books scattered in a ring around me like
warding runes, I knew they could not keep me in blissful
isolation for real, or forever. I think it's the determined firmness with which I sealed myself inside the shelter of fiction
that makes so many of the books I read at that time blur together. It almost didn't matter what world I was retreating to
inside any given book, as long as I could leave my body where
it was, sitting in my bedroom with the door closed, shutting
out the shouting or—sometimes worse—the cold, watchful
silence radiating up the stairs, waiting to be broken. All those
books thatched together to keep me insulated from every-

thing outside the door. But I knew even then that the shelter they offered was small and fragile. A necessary illusion of safety.

*

Not long after I'd made my cards, I had my first experience of another kind of immersive reading. This time, it was not the kind of book I wanted to escape *to,* but rather, a book I couldn't escape *from.* It was unlike anything I'd read before—terrifying, unexpected, essential.

Sometime in high school, I think in tenth or eleventh grade, my class was assigned Toni Morrison's *The Bluest Eye.* The patchiness of my memory here is exactly the opposite of my forgotten childhood readings. I remember everything about what it felt like to read as a child—where I would sit, the quality of light and warmth at different times of year, even the smell of paper dust rising from the page—but very little of the content. With *The Bluest Eye,* though, I can't remember anything about the circumstances of that first reading. I can't recall who my English teacher was that year, or how it was presented to us, nor can I remember reading it at home, or in between the end of class and the beginning of track practice, or on the bus to a meet. I can't remember if I talked to anyone about this book, or if I ever said anything about how it got inside me. Certainly, I never told anyone about how I'd think of it unexpectedly, with a shiver, for years after, or how I was afraid to take it off the shelf to reread but unwilling to get rid of it.

What I do remember, in fine-grained detail, is the book itself. I only read it once back then, yet images from it, even specific phrases, sank immediately into my memory. I can still see certain scenes being played and replayed with astonishing clarity: the determined destruction of a ghastly pink-faced baby doll, little girls struggling with one another in the dry red dirt between two houses, an unkind old white man behind the counter at a run-down corner store straight out of a Depression-era soundstage. A young girl smiling into a mirror at a reflection only she can see. Marigold seeds that will never grow, planted by small hands in cold ground.

The moment I remember most clearly and most often is from the end of the book. The novel tells the story of Pecola Breedlove, an outcast, abused, young Black girl in 1930s Lorain, Ohio. Through the eyes of Claudia and Frieda, her sometime allies, readers witness a string of events that drive Pecola, already excluded, even further outside the social world of the neighborhood, and finally into a self-protective state of madness. After the very worst has befallen her—raped by her father, pregnant, shunned by the town, maligned and uncared for—Pecola prays for the one thing she believes can somehow save her and make everyone love her: the bluest, most beautiful pair of eyes in the world. The last time we see her is also the only time we hear her internal monologue—actually a dialogue between her divided selves, the Pecola who believes that her wish has been granted and that her eyes have turned the bluest blue, and a mysterious "friend" who speaks to her and stays with her as nobody else will. The premise is tragic and frightening on its own, but it's hard to put a finger on exactly what makes the conversation between Pecola and not-Pecola so terrifying. Perhaps it is the blissful certainty of the lost girl, sure both of her new, blue eyes, and of her new, invisible friend. Perhaps it is the sudden, direct access to her mind, which, until now, has been in the third person, knowable only through the coy half mediation of free indirect discourse. Obviously—no perhaps here—it is the horror of how Pecola arrived here, driven deep into herself by the same violent myths of beauty and goodness and safety (all the provinces of whiteness) that her madness upholds. When I first read it, at fifteen or sixteen, I was not ready or able to articulate this last horror. But the line that stuck in my mind, that alarmed me so much, is telling. It was something Pecola, preening over her new eyes, says to her imaginary companion: "You're just jealous."

"You're just jealous." Strange for such petty words to be so haunting. I couldn't say exactly what frightened me about them. Now, it's so clear that it had to do with all those characters I'd designed so painstakingly, page after page of self-effacing wishes, faces I wished were mine. If I'd woken up one day and found myself miraculously transformed into one of my beautiful, devil-may-care, large-eyed heroines, that's exactly what I would have said, with casual cruelty, to whatever cringing shred of the old Sarah that lingered: "You're just jealous."

Being unequipped at the time to make even this obvious therapeutic insight, I couldn't pin down what it was that terrified me so much about *The Bluest Eye* in that first reading. There are overtly traumatic events in the book, but the only ones I could identify were things I understood objectively to be terrible. My sheltered classmates and I were at least educated in the basic facts of what is patently unbearable, like sexual violence, incest, and the surface-level signs of traditional American racism. What I had not been taught to process, however, was precisely what made this book so intimately devastating, a condition of being that I recognized, but could not bear to confront: the stinging impossibility of being beautiful or good in a world where beauty and goodness shone most brightly out of the biggest, bluest eyes.

To say that I "identified" with Pecola is not only reductive, but self-dramatizing. Pecola is a poor Black girl growing up in an abusive, tormented family warped by personal and historical violence in small-town 1930s Ohio; I was a middle-class Japanese girl growing up in a medium-troubled immigrant family in suburban Ohio circa Y2K. The only thing we shared was a geographical association. But nonetheless, I *felt* something in Pecola, a profound recognition that I experienced as too real and very dangerous. This recognition was a far cry from the warm embrace of relatability that readers often seek from sympathetic characters. Pecola's wish for the bluest eyes, and her dissociative belief that she has received them, jabbed a bruise I did not know I had. I recognized the shape of her hopeless and intense desire, a shape that felt instinctively familiar, as if I could trace its razor-edged curves with my own dark, narrow eyes squeezed shut.

*

I had one recurring dream all through high school and college. It would keep the narrative ends so neatly tied and trimmed if I could definitively say that it started when I read Morrison, but I don't think it did. In the dream I was always in the bathroom at home, standing in front of the big mirror, lit from above by late-afternoon sun through the skylight. The light was beautiful and hazy, dancing with dust motes. In my left hand I held some kind of knife—I can't remember exactly how it was shaped, but its warm handle fit my palm snugly, and I knew without checking that the edge was magically keen. Calmly and without fear, I'd cut away the excess parts of my body. The knife slid through my flesh smoothly, without resistance, like wire through clay—a painless, satisfying feeling. I was my own artwork. With two confident flicks of the blade, I hollowed a space between my thighs. Long, graceful strokes skimmed the undersides from my upper arms. The flesh fell away in spiraling ribbons, falling around my feet like hair at a salon. A slimmer, longer neck would be revealed, intersected neatly by a clean, sharp jaw. I never got to my face—I do not think I had one. The last cuts I'd make were at the waist: two arcing, elegant swoops that descended from rib to hip. These last pieces to fall were immediately hilarious. All of a sudden, the scene became absurd, and instead of making art, it was like carving a Thanksgiving turkey. I always laughed.

It was not a nightmare. If anything, it was a good dream. I don't think I worried about whether this kind of dream was normal or healthy, because it was so unexceptional. Are anyone's dreams normal or healthy? Probably not. I do remember knowing that it was not the kind of thing you should tell anyone about. It went into the deep quarry that held all the things I refused to think about, like the memory of that plate smashing into the kitchen wall, or the chant that my elementary school nemesis used to sing at recess (the old classic: "Chinese, Japanese, dirty knees, look at these"). Some of these things were stirred up by *The Bluest Eye,* and that disturbance was alarming. I didn't know if these things could be cast back into the depths once they bobbed up to the surface.

There are a lot of self-evident connections between the things in the quarry that I didn't make then, not because I didn't know they were there, but because I could not bear to see them made. In this case, an obvious thread strings together the cards, *The Bluest Eye,* and the dream. Put side by side, these elements are consistent and can lead to an ordinary conclusion, which is that I was just a girl who was unhappy with her appearance. At the time, I would have scoffed at this idea. Instead, I had a carefully cultivated explanation that, I believed, made perfect, undeniable sense. You can come up with such persuasive backstories for self-loathing. I was convinced that my fixation on perfecting my physical form, and the ambitious patterns of disordered eating that came with it, were purely pragmatic. I wanted to be thinner so I would be lighter; I wanted to be lighter so I could run faster; I wanted to run faster so I could prove I was a leader by putting "team captain" on my college applications and getting in to one of my reach schools. It was so very obvious to me that the rest of my life depended on the loss of eight or ten stubborn pounds. The fact that my parents wanted this for me made it seem like a simple fact of life. We three all believed that the body was as perfectible as the future.

I could make myself understand why I needed to work on disciplining and correcting my physique, but this admissions-based pseudoscience could not explain why my face also upset me so much. I couldn't diet my face away; it was, I supposed, just plain ugly, a fact I accepted with an unquestioning resignation. If I could correct my body, I thought—and by extension everything else—it might at least mitigate this unresolvable situation. Pecola's wish raised the perturbing suspicion that there was a reason for my hatred of my face greater than just my particular features. But I couldn't bear to think through that suspicion, especially if it churned up unresolvable problems that would muddy the clear logic of reduction and discipline that ruled my daily life, a clarity that needed to be maintained for me to keep treading water.

Here's another extremely obvious connection from that time that I simply could not make: The song I listened to on repeat most often when I was alone in my room was Björk's "Hyperballad."

> We live on a mountain
> Right at the top
> This beautiful view
> From the top of the mountain.
> Every morning, I walk towards the edge
> And throw little things off
> Like car parts, bottles, and cutlery
> Or whatever I find lying around.

I go through all this, sings Björk, *before you wake up / So I can feel happier to be safe up here with you.* No lyrics could describe what I was up to more precisely than these, but I just couldn't see it. It's mortifying to be so predictable, to have the pieces of one's past fit together so perfectly into a mosaic of the present, like a character in a bad novel, or, in fact, like one of the fantasy characters of my own design. There were so many things I needed to cast over the edge of my mountain just to stay up there, willfully ignorant and supposedly safe. Looking back, it seems like all I did was toss things out over the edge, looking down to see them disappear into darkness, not yet realizing that they always come back.

Björk was proximate to one of these things. I'd bought this album, *Post*, not because I was a cool record store kid with a precocious ear for avant-garde pop, but because of Kristi Yamaguchi, who'd skated a flirty exhibition routine to the single "It's Oh So Quiet." When I was an Olympics-obsessed baby figure skater, Kristi had been everything to me. She was a skater and a Japanese person who was accepted as an American—one thing I already was, and another I felt like I couldn't be. I adored her big eyes that stayed bright and open, even when she smiled her biggest smile with her big white teeth; my eyes folded up and disappeared if I smiled, a fact that did not go unremarked by my classmates. I generally tried not to smile. She was perfect and beautiful and popular and nobody on TV ever seemed surprised that she spoke unaccented Northern Californian English. She was the first real role model I had, and after she turned pro and mostly disappeared from the public eye, I quit skating and quit hoping to find another. I eventually tossed my skates over the edge of the cliff, and Kristi with them. I kept the Björk CD, though.

I haven't thought of Kristi for years. I've just clawed my way out of a YouTube crevasse of her skating routines, which brought sudden, confusing tears to my eyes, as I realized that my first period of real, deep depression set in right about when I abandoned her. These tears were stopped in their tracks by the video that autoplayed after her Albertville short program, an excruciating PSA called "Hip to Be Fit with Kristi Yamaguchi and the California Raisins."

I'm stalling here.

The other strand that ran through those years—from the cards, to the knife dream, to the quarry of actively forgotten things, to *The Bluest Eye*—was cutting. Call it a habit, call it a vocation, call it self-harm or self-soothing: I did not call it anything. It was just a thing I did, as matter-of-factly as brushing my teeth. I kept a packet of razor blades hidden behind a tangled mess of hair ties and butterfly clips in one of my bathroom drawers but preferred a knife when I could sneak one upstairs from the kitchen; my dad had been a restaurant cook in a past life and kept his knives so sharp that their edges felt like whispers. I was accustomed, then addicted, to what little pain there was. I loved how clean, straight lines traced carefully across the surface of my skin were the only thing that could render me—or at least, these hidden parts of me—suddenly so beautiful in their elegant geometry, their precision and control. I wished everyone could look at them and see how perfect I could be.

It seems so stupid now to say that I honestly never thought about the cutting in the context of these other troubling things, not even that extremely literal-minded dream. It was so ordinary that I did not even notice as I unthinkingly made all the calculations and adjustments that any avid self-harmer must, learning from past mistakes to apply the blade to unseen places, like the upper thigh or torso, and how to stay quiet and change fast in the locker room before practice. I simply would not let myself see how all these habits linked up obliquely.

But there's no point beating myself up about this now; unseeing is one of the great pastimes of adolescence. I also can't imagine that my peers and I managed to come away with a very nuanced understanding of Morrison's novel or the way it revealed an America not so terribly distant from our class-

room, temporally or geographically. I read it, like everything
then, as young people often do, through the tiny frame of my
own small life. All the same, perhaps because of that myopia,
The Bluest Eye did something unexpected to me. For the first
time, peering through it back at myself, I briefly saw and then
could not ever fully unsee the taut web that connected all my
harmful practices of survival—and how they might be an-
chored in the world.

*

A few years ago, I got very interested in the idea that everyone
who is incurably obsessed with books has a Life Ruiner. The
Life Ruiner is the book that sets you on the path to a life built
by and around reading. To call it a Life Ruiner is not to say
that a life of letters is necessarily ruination—but rather, to
identify it as the book you can't ever recover from, that you
never stop thinking about, and that makes you desperate to
reach that frightening depth of experience with other books.
A Life Ruiner can be a text you are constantly rereading, or a
text you've lost forever and are always seeking. It's the book
that will not let you go. It is a book that starts you on a quest,
but not a quest that will end in resolution or salvation—rather,
a grail quest like the actual Arthurian Grail quest, that can
only end in dissolution and further mystery. After you encounter a Life Ruiner, your reading is altered in ways you may
not realize until you've read ten or a hundred other books and
found that you cannot return to the way you read before, or
perhaps the way you thought or lived before. I think of the
Life Ruiner as the book that first gave you the hot impulse to

keep pursuing whatever it was that astounded you about it, to keep peering at it even if it made you feel like your brain was melting, like staring into the sun.

For a while, I went around asking all my book-centric friends what their Life Ruiners were. The question provoked some laughter and a little confusion but pretty much all of them came up with answers almost immediately. My colleague Russ was the first to turn the question back on me, as we lurked in the entryway of our basement offices, smoking illicit cigarettes out of the view of our clean-living students. I hadn't thought about mine before posing the question to him, but as soon as he asked, I knew that it was *The Bluest Eye*.

Morrison's novel ruined me in more ways than one. On the readerly front, it was a powerful relic I treated with deference and awe, like a saint's wristbone. I carried that paperback copy with me through eleven moves, across the Atlantic and back, to the West Coast and back, one of a very few permanent fixtures on my shelves all the way through high school, college, and graduate school. It was a talisman, and I knew I should never let it out of my sight, even though I was too afraid to reread it and feel again the way it had made me feel. When I first read it, I couldn't understand how or why, but I knew that this book was different from anything I had read before. Morrison's descriptions curled in my mind and lashed out to my nerve endings. Of course, I had come across plenty of lovely words and enchanting phrases in many of the books I'd read up to that point, especially the ones I read over and over again. But this was different. Somehow the jarring beauty of the language, metaphor after metaphor sinuously winding around the vital terror that the book inspired, imbued the book itself with a kind of electrical charge. Ever since, every time I pulled it from a moving box, or accidentally came across it on a shelf, I felt a static shock I could have sworn was physical. I've now read many of Morrison's other novels, and they have thrilled me and taught me and frightened me, but none of them tore at me the same unexpected way *The Bluest Eye* did. The Life Ruiner had done its work.

But *The Bluest Eye* did more than change the way I read literature—it also made it impossible for me to read my own circumstances as I had before. The novel forced me to look deep down into those thoughts and feelings I tried so hard never to examine, as well as into the history of the specific place I lived in and the country my family and I still thought of as foreign.

The thoughts and feelings I'd buried the deepest were about race. For as long as I could remember, I had tried not to remind the people I knew—who, by the time I reached high school, were mostly white—that I was not like them. As what my Canadian passport form calls a "visible minority," though, that decision was not up to me. When I was very young, that visibility made me, already shy and prone to social terror, even shyer and more terrified. As I grew older, I tried very hard not to dwell on this difference myself, hoping that my own studied nonchalance about race would rub off on my peers. I just tried to put my head down and not show my face. I did not smile; I tried to keep my eyes as open as they would go. I assiduously avoided Asian content outside of the home. When my father half-proudly and half-angrily called me a banana, I was hurt, but secretly a little jubilant: It was working. I was whitening—not on the outside, but on the inside, which

surely counted for something. Surely someone could see it—
a glint of cobalt flashing deep within my black eyes.

My encounter with the novel made it harder to maintain
my willful, pernicious blindness to the way that people saw
me—and the way they talked about race around me—that I'd
cultivated for so long. Even so, I kept smiling blankly through
the early 2000s, the era of ironic, Urban Outfitters racism,
taking nonsense Engrish jokes as the cost of admission to
white adjacency. I tried to be patient when a companion tried
to convince me that he called me "Ching Pong" as an endear-
ment and when two friends—we were so close at the time
that they referred to themselves as my husbands—asked earnestly if I could see less out of my tiny, squinty eyes. I hate
thinking of how many times I turned a tiny blind eye to all
manner of jokey jibes—aimed at me and, worse, at others—
rendered more stinging by the misguided fondness with
which they were delivered. Or, worst of all, I often did not
even see them. These were the mechanisms of active forget-
ting that I engaged in, both consciously and unconsciously.
Like cutting, they seemed so ordinary. And, like cutting, it
didn't hurt to perform these actions, at least not in a way that
I recognized as hurt. To look directly at these behaviors would
have ripped that hurt up from wherever it was hiding, made it
blossom and spread.

Pecola's desire for transformation pressed on those wounds
and made that pain flare up, sharper and more acute than I
could have imagined. I responded by closing the book firmly
but not letting it go. When I think of it now, the way I dealt
with this Life Ruiner makes perfect sense and no sense at all.
I could not bear to go back to it, because it would have made
it impossible to continue with my routines of self-denial and

self-rejection. But it also makes no sense that I, a curious and hungry reader who wanted to be a writer, could have resisted the urge to go back in and see what it did to me on a second or third reading and learn how it worked, instead of just carting it around with me for all that time.

*

Recently, I returned to *The Bluest Eye*, after more than twenty years. It was so strange to take it down from the shelf and turn it over in my hands. My copy looked nearly new, despite the fact that it had been traveling with me since high school. The violet gloss is worn off here and there along the still-sharp edges of its spine, and the far corners of its covers are ever so slightly rounded, but it is otherwise unmarred and uncreased. Its spine is not even cracked—I had been trained well by my brother, a meticulous guardian of paperbacks and comic books, in the art of treating every book with a respect verging on idolatry, a faith from which I've lapsed. I sat for a long moment, just looking at the closed book. To open it again after all this time felt unwisely like inviting in a ghost. I half expected a gust of icy wind and a flurry of cobwebs to rush out when I lifted the cover.

I had remembered Pecola's final dissociation, but I had forgotten that the novel begins with chaotic disintegration, as well. It starts with a paragraph from a *Dick and Jane* primer: "Here is the house. It is green and white. It has a red door. It is very pretty. Here is the family. Mother, Father, Dick, and Jane live in the green-and-white house. They are very happy." And so on.

The paragraph repeats, this time without punctuation:

"Here is the house it is green and white it has a red door it is very pretty."

And again, without spaces: "Hereisthehouseitisgreenand whiteithasareddooritisverypretty."

The anxiety it provokes is palpable. I had to take a break after these first two pages. I'd been expecting something stressful, but not this tumbling onslaught. The device is so simple and so immediately effective, an instant breakdown of so many things at once: language, sanity, trust. I admired it and felt a little dizzy.

It was not just this efficient demolition of Dick and Jane's world that made me woozy—there was another surprise. I had expected a pristine text, as unmarked as the book's cover, but when I turned to it, the first page was covered in neat, careful writing; I remembered belatedly that my English teachers had required that we make annotations. I wrote mine with the most nineties adolescent implement possible, a neon cantaloupe gel pen, and over the years the paper had yellowed enough to make the words almost invisible. Flipping forward, I saw that I switched to a metallic silver on page 122, which is only slightly more legible. I felt like an archaeologist deciphering the layers of a palimpsest.

My notes were humbling, revealing teenage me to be nowhere near as clever or precocious as I had fancied myself— just banal phrases like "fiction vs. reality," "HAPPY FAMILY," "American Dream." My favorite of the annotations on the first Dick and Jane page is a chart with two columns, clearly the remnants of an unsuccessful in-class exercise. One is labeled "Ideal" and the other "Real," under which heading I'd listed things like "violence?," "taxes," and "day care," which paint a surprisingly accurate picture of adult life.

Continuing through the novel, it was impossible not to be distracted by these traces of me from the past. They dragged on my rereading; every time I came across a phrase in the margin, or a section starred and underlined, I had to stop and investigate it. The questions and observations I wrote were all just as obvious, but the more obscure marks became more and more interesting to me as the book went on. From the beginning, alongside my pedestrian thoughts on historical context and literary devices ("FORESHADOWING!"), certain passages are just underlined, with no comment. It's sometimes hard to tell what I saw in them or how much I could have seen. As an adult, thinking about what things were like when I first read it, my breath caught when I read Claudia's description of how she can't stop crying when her mother's anger "humiliates" her—yet, writing from beyond childhood, she asks herself, "But was it really like that? As painful as I remember? Only mildly. Or rather, it was a productive and fructifying pain." I had to ask myself the same thing: Was it as painful as I remember, as painful as I'm telling you it was? I had drawn a careful star in the margin. Had I guessed that someday I, like Claudia, would find myself questioning the truth of memory? Or did I intuit that whatever pain there was would ultimately prove "productive and fructifying," and its fruit would feed everything I'd do or write?

There are also passages I think I must have marked purely for their beauty. I can almost remember what I felt, or at least imagine how I might have felt, reading these words:

Their conversation is like a gently wicked dance: sound meets sound, curtsies, shimmies, and retires. Another sound enters but is upstaged by still another: the two circle each other and stop. Sometimes their words move in lofty spirals; other times they take strident leaps, and all of it is punctuated with warm-pulsed laughter—like the throb of a heart made of jelly.

Reading it reminds me of the first stirrings of the desire to really write, when I would stay up late and tear through page after page of my journal, groping around for the words that pulsed warm like that laughter, "like the throb of a heart made of jelly," words that made me feel alive.

But the markings that really intrigue me are the most vehement ones, words or sentences that have been underlined heavily and with uncharacteristic sloppiness, sometimes so many times that the lines almost slice through the page. They are the ones that hit most directly at the heart of the matter. Returning to the text, Morrison's argument against idealized physical beauty, and its association with goodness— "Probably the most destructive ideas in the history of human thought"—is far more overt than I'd remembered. There is no way, even given the rudimentary state of my observational skills, that I could not have connected the obvious dots here, between Claudia's narration of her indoctrination into the cruel racket of what is "beautiful" and my own. When she describes her resentment of Shirley Temple as "unsullied hatred," I had drawn a careful box around the words for emphasis. Alongside her description of the annual gift of a "blue-eyed, yellow-haired, pink-skinned doll" for Christmas, which adults assume to be every Black child's "fondest wish," I had written

"BEAUTY"
White

I wish I could touch this message and somehow be sent back into whatever I was feeling when I penned those words. A couple of pages later, Claudia explains her wish to dissect the dolls and discover, as though by science, what made them so lovable to the adults and older girls around her. When eventually she "learned how repulsive this disinterested violence was, that it was repulsive because it was disinterested, [her] shame floundered about for refuge. The best hiding place was love. Thus the conversion from pristine sadism to fabricated hatred, to fraudulent love." This whole passage is underlined, but the words "pristine sadism" are scarred with extra vigor, double and triple underlined, with a messy star gesturing to them from the margin. I'm not sure if I was afraid of, or inspired by, the child's "unsullied" and "pristine" rejection of what society called beauty, and if I wanted to return to that state of nature or remind myself not to give in to it. I wish I could know.

Another passage that I marked with violent enthusiasm appears a little later, as two classmates, also Black, are taunting Pecola for her family's poverty and blackness. As Claudia narrates,

It was their contempt for their own blackness that gave the first insult its teeth. They seemed to have taken all of their smoothly cultivated ignorance, their exquisitely learned self-hatred, their elaborately designed hopelessness and sucked it all up into a fiery cone of scorn that

had burned for ages in the hollows of their minds—
cooled—and spilled over lips of outrage, consuming
whatever was in its path.

I unsteadily underlined the whole paragraph from which
these lines are taken, and scrawled a message in the margin
that is so self-evident that I wonder why I felt like I had to
replicate it: "HATE THEMSELVES." Did I understand
then that I also might have written "HATE MYSELF"
alongside the words "smoothly cultivated ignorance ... exquisitely learned self-hatred ... elaborately designed hopelessness"? (I suddenly remember how I laughed louder than
anyone else watching Mickey Rooney's yellowface grotesque-
rie in *Breakfast at Tiffany's* at a middle school sleepover.) Or
did I let myself off the hook because of the distance offered by
the distinction of "their own blackness," which was, I understood even then, somehow different from what my father an-
grily insisted on calling our own yellowness? (Even though he
has lost his speech now, his voice is still hissing in my ear:
Don't you ever forget, to those hakujin *you are always just yellow.*)
How much could I have understood at that point, living in a
predominantly white place, about how those categories might
speak to one another?

Morrison is very specific about the fact that, in crafting the
language of *The Bluest Eye,* she is writing to and for Black
culture and language. As she writes in the 1993 afterword,

My choices of language (speakerly, aural, colloquial), my
reliance for full comprehension on codes embedded in
black culture, my effort to effect immediate co-conspiracy

and intimacy (without any distancing, explanatory fabric), as well as my attempt to shape a silence while breaking it are attempts to transfigure the complexity and wealth of Black-American culture into a language worthy of the culture.

Furthermore, she emphasizes the conditions of Pecola's life, remarking that "in trying to dramatize the devastation that even casual racial contempt can cause, [she] chose a unique situation, not a representative one." However, despite the specificity and extremity of Pecola's life, Morrison still "believed some aspects of her woundability were lodged in all young girls." I can remember some of the experience of this woundability but I can only wonder how much of it, if any, I understood.

Then there's a passage that is notable for its clean, unmarked quality; the pages that surround it are peppered with notes and markings, but it is conspicuously untouched, despite its importance to the novel's characterization of Pecola. Reading it now, I feel a chilling, familiar thrill of recognition. Doubly familiar, because I can suddenly recall the first time I read this paragraph, and also because it describes in precise terms one of my own childhood habits. Following a terrible brawl between her mother, father, and brother, Pecola hides in bed under a quilt, feeling sick and afraid.

"Please, God," she whispered into the palm of her hand. "Please make me disappear." She squeezed her eyes shut. Little parts of her body faded away. Now slowly, now with a rush. Slowly again. Her fingers went, one by one;

then her arms disappeared all the way to the elbow. Her
feet now. Yes, that was good. The legs all at once. It was
hardest above the thighs. She had to be real still and
pull. Her stomach would not go. But finally it, too, went
away. Then her chest, her neck. The face was hard, too.
Almost done, almost. Only her tight, tight eyes were left.
They were always left.

I was familiar with this kind of desperate meditation practice. I spent what seems now like a lot of time lying very still
in bed. First, I'd be listening with my whole body, trying to
hear what my parents were fighting about downstairs. Then,
when they were done, I'd stay as still as I could, waiting for
one or the other of them to stick their head in the door and
check if I was sleeping. Still as death, I'd lie there, waiting,
wishing that I could disappear, leaving only an empty, lightly
mussed bed for them to discover. Pecola made herself disappear from the hands and feet up, but I always vanished from
the face down. For her, the eyes are the hardest part, "always
left." For me, though, it was like I began without a face—no
eyes at all, and a soft nose, cheeks, mouth that blurred into
one another, just a smooth plaque molded into low planes and
indentations—a sci-fi version of the impassive, masklike face
of the Oriental stereotype. Lying in the dark, it was easy to
imagine a blank expanse where my face should have been, and
that blankness made it easier to feel my heavy torso and limbs
lighten and dissolve from the neck down. Even in daytime,
my face was barely there. I had difficulty recognizing myself
in photographs and struggled to see my face as a cohesive
whole in the mirror, confusions that persist even now. It's ob-

vious why I didn't have to mark that passage. I did not need a reminder of an everyday occurrence.

*

Morrison signs off the afterword with her location and the date: Princeton, New Jersey, November 1993. I moved to Princeton to teach almost exactly twenty years later. Morrison was then a professor emerita, though she had recently moved away, and her mythic presence was still strongly felt. My first year there, I lived just off campus, in a university-owned apartment building that felt discouragingly temporary, like an orphanage for single faculty. I took long, slow runs around town, gawping at the large, beautiful houses occupied by senior faculty and wealthy commuters. I knew that, until recently, Toni Morrison had lived in one of the lovely houses around campus, but I never asked which. One of my colleagues claimed to have walked by Morrison's house one day and seen what was on the TV (*Project Runway,* allegedly). I was excited but intimidated by the past proximity of the great writer; I didn't want to know which house was hers, for fear that I'd get so nervous running by it that I'd trip over my own feet. I knew she wouldn't be there, but I still had the irrational feeling that she could somehow see me, and the only impression I'd ever make on the finest novelist of our age would be of an inept jogger tumbling down the sidewalk and quickly scurrying out of view on all fours.

This paranoid feeling of closeness was a fantasy. I had that feeling we've all had about authors who "get" us, which I knew was ridiculous and self-aggrandizing. Toni Morrison was never going to be my friend. And of course, Morrison didn't write *The Bluest Eye* for me, or even someone like me. It is always foolishness to think that someone has written any book *for* you, though it is a foolishness that can be hard to resist, especially when you're lonely. But still, I wish I could have run into her just once, so I could have told her how important it was for *The Bluest Eye* to ruin my life. How important it is to read a book that so undoes you that it becomes a precious token of your own destruction to carry to the end of your days.

Chapter 4

THE NON-EXISTENT
PELT

We had a canonical rom-com meet-cute in an airport, as I was anxiously headed home for the holidays (cue Bill Nighy drawling "Christ*mas* Is A*roun*d Me"). It wasn't the arrivals gate at Heathrow Airport, but it wasn't far off: the WHSmith in the south terminal at Gatwick, where I discovered that love actually was available in paperback for—as I recall—only £9.99. My flight had been delayed by a snowstorm in Chicago, and I'd already finished the only book in my carry-on, so I was trawling the shelves and tables of the bookstore with the too-deliberate slowness of the marooned traveler killing time. When I saw A. S. Byatt's *Possession*, my breath caught. I didn't find it immediately attractive—the UK paperback edition of the time had an overdressed cover that looked like potpourri smells—but its reputation preceded it. A teacher with whom I'd cultivated a cautious relationship of mutual dislike and respect had recently recommended it to me. She didn't say why I was a good match for it, but rather grandly declared that its last page was one of the saddest things she'd

ever read. I could not for the life of me imagine what was
"sad" to this cold, terrifying woman. As a result, like Emma
Woodhouse meeting Frank Churchill, I'd been nursing a
crush on *Possession* before encountering it in person. Like
theirs, our first actual meeting was inauspicious and facili-
tated by transportation problems.

I was returning from my first semester away from home. I'd
won a scholarship for a year of school in England before starting college—my first escape from the vigilantly enforced con-
straints of my parents' house. I'd had great hopes for instant
transformation, imagining that I would finally become the
devastatingly compelling, wild, brilliant, attractive, all-around
strange and extraordinary person I hadn't been allowed to be
at home. But nearly half the year had gone by and, other than
a weepy navel piercing that refused to heal, I remained sadly
unaltered. At the airport going home for winter break, I was
impatient and jittery; for months, my legs had been twitchy,
like they wanted to run and run until I caught up with my
fascinating future self. Or perhaps I was just tired and bored
after two hours of idly rolling my suitcase back and forth.
Whatever it was, I was all wound up and ready for something,
anything, to happen when I sat down in the smoking lounge,
WHSmith bag rustling in hand. I did not want to retreat
home the same as I had been when I left. I did, at least, feel
smugly like a sophisticated international traveler with a black
coffee, a book of matches, an unopened pack of red Gauloises,
and a long novel laid out on the table next to me. I fiddled
with this arrangement of accoutrements and then picked up
the book.

I was shocked: For once, something *did* happen. The two
hours of delay sped by as I whipped through the pages, light-

ing one cigarette off the last, occasionally turning back to re-read, and I almost missed the boarding call for my flight. I got in the line and read as I stood there, repeatedly annoying the people in line as I let gaps open in front of me, scooting my bag along with my foot so I could hold the book open as I rushed forward, trying to get a few more pages in. Finally in my seat, I turned on my light and settled in, thrilling to the knowledge that there would be nothing to distract my read-ing for the nine-ish hours of the flight. I finished *Possession* as the plane began its descent into Chicago, closed it with a sigh, and shut my eyes as we taxied to the Continental terminal. I did not think that it was the saddest thing I'd ever read. I wasn't sure what to think at all yet. I felt a new oddness. I believed unquestioningly that *it* had happened. I had fallen in love.

What does it mean, to fall in love with a book? I'd been jealously captivated by the worlds of books before, wishing that I could inhabit them forever. I'd been infatuated with characters on occasion, like a predictable little high school crush on Zooey Glass (now insufferable), minor romantic training exercises that never got serious. I'd loved books but not been *in* love with them. This was something else.

Maggie Nelson begins her book *Bluets* with a proposition: "Suppose I were to begin by saying that I had fallen in love with a color." I make a related proposition to you: Suppose I were to begin by saying that I had fallen in love with a novel. "Suppose I were to speak this as though it were a confession," Nelson continues, "suppose I shredded my napkin as we spoke."

"It began slowly. An appreciation, an affinity. Then, one day, it became more serious. Then . . . it became somehow personal.*"*

I could say the same about *Possession*. But I whirled through Nelson's stages of appreciation, affinity, and intimacy, reading it on the plane, immediately delighted by its self-assured multiplicity. I wanted to wrap myself in it, to burrow inside it— not in the scholarly convolutions of the book's plot but really inside the vibrant grain of its texture, the very fibers of its style. Byatt does not take any time to warm up; from the get-go, she starts busily stitching together different genres (lyric and epic poetry, the epistolary novel, campus fiction, fairy tale), dual romantic plotlines that unfold a century apart, perfectly cutting but weirdly tender little character studies, and a wry critique of the academic tendencies of the 1980s, the latter of which I couldn't yet recognize. And best of all, lush, gorgeous passages of unconstrained description. Never had I seen an author delve into the depths of a glorious hidden Yorkshire cove or a stuffy suburban bathroom with such evident, rapturous pleasure. I appreciated it with my whole reading body. I felt a tingling, aspirational affinity. Later I would feel incredibly jealous of it, sometimes infuriated by it; the other things we know to expect from love.

It was just so confident, so flauntingly itself (the most attractive thing in the world, in a person or in a book). This is still one of the things I love most about it—how it boldly, confidently performs both its intimidating intelligence and the gratification of its love of or, better, *lust* for language. It is a book that is unafraid to exercise its ideas to their fullest, longest-winded extent, a quality that, I soon realized, did not endear it to everyone I recommended it to. Perhaps because of this, when I look back to my transatlantic tryst with *Possession*, I can't help but see it with an equal amount of eye-rolling and fondness, as my own version of *Before Sunrise*. I may never have had a night of verbose passion with a turtleneck-wearing young mansplainer on a Eurail pass, but I did have this night of blissful reading with Dame Antonia Susan Byatt.

*

At first, I was sure that to explain my feelings for *Possession*, I'd have to tell the story of the first human being I fell in love with, my college boyfriend. Sophomore year, I dated him for about six months and spent twice as long getting over the breakup—an exemplary first romantic outing, benign but not boring, by turns appropriately ecstatic and tortured, that provided enough material for terrible poetry and maudlin essayistic musings to carry me clear through the end of college. Try as I might, though, I can't get away from the feeling that this first experiment in love was just that: The laboratory conditions were set up in such a way that this reaction was inevitable. I did truly care for him in a way I'd never cared for anyone before. But looking back at it, so many of the feelings this relationship provoked, while it was happening and after, were really distorted versions of the mental and emotional states I was experiencing on my own anyway: loneliness, desire, self-loathing, curiosity. Being with him was like looking at these feelings through a magnifying glass; from some angles, a beam of intensified light could burn away the worst ones, and from others, they loomed obscenely large and terrifyingly clear. I suspect a lot of early loves are like this. The same was true of this first reading of *Possession*.

It is also true that meditating on falling in love—like other such extraordinary and commonplace life events—can be the best way to feel splendidly special but to simultaneously recognize that you are just undergoing the most quotidian aspect of the human condition, or rather, the way humans are conditioned. In this case, as Byatt writes dryly near the end of *Possession*, the conditioning is genre dictated: "The expectations of Romance control almost everyone in the Western world, for better or worse, at some point or another." I realize now that I was thinking of love—of people, of books—in too limited a way, as only the most commonplace definition of the word "Romance."

I'd always suspected, with the thoughtlessness of a child who has always been sure that she was loved (even if in a too-intense and damaging way), that love had to be romantic to really count. Romance, I thought, must be what made love worth it. The familial love I knew was a painful, unbalanced burden rather than a source of pleasure or comfort. *Real* love, I thought, would instantaneously transport me to the real life I was destined for. My dramatic encounter with *Possession* enabled this suspicion to bloom suddenly into certainty, like time-lapse footage of a rose. I'd pined for the idea of a big, bombastic romance for a long time but had not allowed myself to hope that I could have it; in high school, I'd been certain that I would never find what I was looking for in suburban Ohio, so I never even tried. Once I was out of my parents' house and across the ocean, I'd begun to hope that life could change—everything I had not let myself desire suddenly seemed possible. When *Possession* hit me—like a bolt of lightning, like a ray of sunlight through the clouds, like an annoyingly apt cliché—it confirmed this hope. If it could happen with a book, it could happen with a person. I knew for sure that love was out there; that life was out there. What I could not see was that I was too much in love with the idea of being in love, with a book, with a person, with anything or anyone, to actually realize that life was happening all along.

Romantic love seems so unique, so singular—so stupidly exceptional. And indeed, one of the "expectations of Romance" that *Possession* itself set me up for was the idea that love should be small-*r* romantic. But that's not the only thing Byatt means when she invokes that overdetermined term. The genre of Romance is as much about pursuit itself as the pursuit of a highly specific vision of love—the desire to achieve some kind of possession. This could be of the divine or the self or the other, depending on whether one is looking at the chivalric romance or the emotional intensity of the Romantic poets or indeed the pathological compulsion to coupledom of the romance plot as we know it.

What *Possession* awakened in me was something I couldn't yet understand: the tentative desire for a quest that will never end, an ever-striving desire that cannot be fulfilled, a pleasurably futile search for complete knowledge of the other that can never be attained—and yet—we cannot stop trying. At best, I think, this is what people seek in romantic relationships. But though there are romantic intrigues that structure *Possession*'s plot and pacing, this novel's true "Romance" is built around a different unending quest, the endless venture of literary study. It's not just a book *about* particular scholars trying to get closer to scholarly discovery; it strains to make the reader experience their desire to keep searching. I couldn't have put this yearning into words then. It was a curiously tender, hard-to-place feeling, like a bruised internal organ. The best I can do now is say that it made me want to want indefinitely.

*

The other thing this reading awakened in me was an undue and strange self-confidence in the potential of my own thought. It sounds melodramatic to say so, but that first reading of *Possession* made me think a different life was possible—the "life of the mind," I guess. It was the kind of one-off little miracle, or just a fluke, depending on how you see it, that can lead to wild-eyed zealous conversion. I had been playing writer all through high school; I edited the literary magazine and giddily churned out mannered little poems by hand at home every night, but I still felt like a fake—somebody had to play that role at every high school, and it fell to me. Senior year I might as well have purged my closet of everything but berets and turtlenecks (a look I wore often, with the confused semi-irony characteristic of the time). I half-heartedly played a lot of roles in those years, trying to find one that felt comfortable; this was just the one that I liked best. I read a vast quantity of fiction, but I didn't challenge myself that much. *The Bluest Eye* remained the most viscerally jarring—frightening, beautiful— thing I'd read, and I freaked out and didn't know how to handle it. I read some of the things I thought the editor of the literary magazine should read. I remember there being a lot of Woolf that I claimed to love but didn't really get at all. I made a big deal of acting like I knew things about poetry. But I just wanted to disappear inside a juicy novel and plow through it as fast as possible, simultaneously hoping it would last forever. Disappearing this way often didn't involve thinking—or rather, nothing I understood as thinking yet. I was a voracious reader, but in that thoughtless, gobbling mode that Brecht calls "culinary." I did not learn to love thinking in high school. There were two categories of knowable experience that I knew I enjoyed at that time: either excelling at things or escaping from them. Nobody had asked me to really *dwell* in thought yet—a third category—myself included. The closest thing I knew to this activity was the kind of obsessive, intrusive worry and fear that plagued me when I couldn't sleep or sat alone for too long without a book or a friend and that terrified me; it was certainly not an activity I sought out, though it sought me out all too often.

But falling into this reading of *Possession* really made me want to think. It invited me to do so in a way that was intimidating and seductive at once. The book was obviously written with a scholar's care and obsession. The *work* in it was visible, and the author's pleasure at doing this work was obvious as well: When Byatt uses the word "glaucous" to describe the chilly shine of a green glass bathroom sink, you feel her luxuriate in the sound, in the way it glances off the reflective face of the basin. With its impressive depth of allusion and breath-holding length of description, the novel puts its readers through their paces playfully, and I found myself elatedly gamboling along, knowing I was tripping over lots of things but still able to keep up. It was fun. It was new. It was hard, but it did not make me feel like a pretender the way that *To the Lighthouse* had a few years before. Instead, it weirdly made me intuit that I was figuring something out that might put me in better stead with *To the Lighthouse* later. I did something I almost never did unless asked to explicitly by a teacher—I immediately, repeatedly reread certain passages at a word-by-word crawl, not to understand what happened, but to figure out how it was happening—for the characters, but also for me and for whoever was writing. I discovered another kind of pleasure reading, the kind that's also joyful work.

I have always been too enamored of virtuosity. This is probably due to early and frequent VHS viewings of *Amadeus*, one of the films—and one of the few topics full stop—that all four members of my family agreed upon. I wanted badly to believe myself capable of being virtuosic at something, *anything*, but had not so far found my area of grace. Though I was genuinely dedicated to certain things—cross-country and track, choral music, calorie counting, real or metaphorical beret-wearing— over the course of high school I became sickeningly aware that I would never be exceptional. I would not be the fastest or the thinnest or the coolest. I was either the worst at being the best, or the best at being okay—a solidly middling member of the varsity squad playing the vicious sport of adolescent life.

Byatt's flamboyant virtuosity was part of what immediately drew me to *Possession*. Expertise is at the heart of its plot and its spiritual concerns, and that thematic throughline plays out in its telling. Its two protagonists, Roland Michell and Maud Bailey, are both young academics, one an unhappily semi-employed research assistant, the other a rising star in the pro-fessoriate. They are brought together by Roland's discovery of a secret correspondence between their objects of study and obsession, the Victorian poets Randolph Henry Ash and Christabel LaMotte. Roland and Maud's love story develops slowly, with not a little resistance, as the two trace the obscured steps of the dead poets. We discover the Victorian love story alongside the scholars, as they read through a series of texts, starting with the newfound letters, then going back to the poems they know so well, using Roland's encyclopedic knowledge of Ash's work, and Maud's of LaMotte's, to find textual evidence for the long-ago extratextual romance. As such, the novel relies upon the strength of long—very, very long—passages of poetry supposedly written by Ash and LaMotte. Of course, these poets are none other than Byatt herself. This is a risky move, contingent upon the idea that a reader might mistake the poems for genuine Victoriana, or, even better, be floored by Byatt's daring and prowess in taking on such a technical challenge. The poems are very believable, sometimes accurately clumsy, often beautiful, and occasionally more memorable than many authentic poems of the period. The book, in short, is a marvel, impressive and fun and irresistible to a certain kind of reader.

These things all spoke to me; they made me feel smarter and made me feel like I had to become smarter still—or at least, more widely read—to fully understand the book's multitudinous network of allusions. *Possession* had an edge of eyebrow-raising provocation about it that I found hard to pin down, as though the book itself (it's narrated in an especially coy omniscient third person) was occasionally looking to see if I was getting its jokes. Much of the novel is related with a sense of measured, knowing restraint, by turns arch and ironic, or taut with sexual and textual tension (tensions that are always wrapped up in each other in Byatt's literary worlds). But it was not just the way Byatt loiters in description, or her winking cleverness, or the mind-boggling commitment to the Victorian bit, or even the small-*r* romance of the paired love stories that *really* got me and tipped me over from appreciation and affinity to love. It was the other kind of romance that is threaded through *Possession* in different hues and textures, over and over again—the love of readers for texts, and for reading itself. It was this that made me feel like I understood some essential part of this book completely—and that it understood me, too.

With my instant appreciation of Byatt's dazzling performance and the affinity I felt for the textual romance at the center of the novel, I finally began to get a hint of where my own potential for virtuosity might lie. I'd always done well in English class—I almost never spoke up, but I made up for it in the copiousness of my writing, and I was a dab hand at imitating the right voices to impress teachers and exam readers. So far, though, I'd not understood that close reading was a thing, especially not something that you could be meaningfully good at. In my test-oriented education, we were trained to notice details and call them symbols, in a heavy-handed, necessarily limited way. I'd enjoyed the extended game of pin the tail on the metaphor that took up most of my precollege education in literature; I also felt instinctively, though uncertainly, that I knew more about the books we read than I could say and liked the chance in papers or essay questions to try and explain why. But I didn't yet see reading itself as a creative act.

Possession changed that. At its end, amid the hubbub of the book's hectic denouement, Roland escapes for a solitary evening to his flat to be alone with his thoughts; to imagine a future, to meditate on the past. There, he returns to Ash, alone with the poet he loves and who he thought he knew so well.

He goes back to one of the poems "for perhaps the twelfth, or maybe even the twentieth, time, a poem he 'knew' in the sense that he had already experienced all its words, in their order, and also out of order, in memory, in selective quotation or misquotation." But there is something different about this repeated reading. This time, the text is *newly* alive, and in reading it, Roland comes alive in a new way, too:

> Now and then there are readings that make the hairs on the neck, the non-existent pelt, stand on end and tremble, when every word burns and shines hard and clear and infinite and exact, like stones of fire, like points of stars in the dark—readings when the knowledge that we *shall know* the writing differently or better or satisfactorily, runs ahead of any capacity to say what we know, or how. In these readings, a sense that the text has appeared to be wholly new, never before seen, is followed, almost immediately, by the sense that it was *always there*, that we the readers, knew it was always there, and have *always known* it was as it was, though we have now for the first time recognised, become fully cognisant of, our knowledge.

Something in this reading transforms Roland, or perhaps awakens a part of himself that had been long dormant. Schooled in the days of high literary theory, "he had been taught that language was essentially inadequate, that it could never speak what was there, that it only spoke itself." Now, though, language lights up and comes alive inside him: "What had happened to him was that the ways in which it *could* be said had become more interesting than the idea that it could not." With this revelation, Roland realizes that his reading has finally opened out to creation. Language begins not only to act on him but to act *in* him, and his mind fills with un-written poems—with a new way of thinking and being.

And reading this passage for the first time, in the dark somewhere over Maine or New Hampshire, I too felt differ-ently alive. I felt just as the words dictated—like these lines had always been there, waiting for me and for anyone who could truly read them, and simultaneously like the words were being written as I read them, perhaps that they were coming into being for me and me alone. I felt a prickle along the back of my neck, the quivering of "the non-existent pelt." I'll never forget the solemn mystery of the feeling. It was like this pas-sage opened an unnoticed door into a new chamber of my heart, or my brain, or a shortcut between the two. I didn't know if it had just appeared, or if it had always been there, a primordial part of my being. Suddenly it was clear to me that books did not work on everyone the way they worked on me, on Roland, on A. S. Byatt. I knew in that moment that I was truly *a reader,* and that that meant something more than I'd ever realized: That was the identity I had been looking for this whole time. I was enraptured by the book itself but equally enraptured with the sense that it gave me someone to be.

I took that new someone back home with me and then worked on figuring out who she was over the next six months in England. By the time I got to college the next September, I hadn't worked out how I should look or act—for some rea-son the turtlenecks had given way to an abundant use of silk scarves as belts, scarves as hair ties, scarves as very small, pre-carious tops—but I did arrive on campus feeling certain that

I had one thing to do: to read as much and as freely as I could, and to believe in that reading, if nothing else.

*

So, I was a reader. But what was the text?

The answer, in college, was everything.* There was nothing, I thought then, that couldn't be read, parsed, and interpreted like a work of literature, not people, not books, not events. This made everything safe and explainable. College felt so big, and I was excited by it, but afraid. People were everywhere, always. Now that it was harder just to shut myself in my room and read fantasy novels all day, blocking out what I could not understand or did not want to, I needed a way to keep things under control, to put up a barrier between myself and these new intrusions. I still had my old ways of feeling safe—the razor blades lived in a Ziploc sandwich bag in my clear plastic shower caddy—but this was otherwise a new topography of experiences and feelings. I quickly realized that you could apply the same techniques to the stories that unfolded every day in real life, as to the things I read for class or, more frequently, in the novels I read while working at the circulation desk in the library, ignoring my assigned reading. You could trace patterns, analyze characters based on their smallest utterances, look for moments when people either intentionally or unintentionally broke the rules of genre. You could make

---

* I was a few years away from encountering Derrida's most famous aphorism, "Il n'y a pas de hors-texte," which can be translated with misleading elegance as "There is nothing outside the text" or more awkwardly and accurately as "There is no outside-the-text." If I had encountered this phrase at that time, I would have glibly misread it and applied it to everything in life.

arguments and bolster them with the textual evidence of everyday life, and those arguments could become the laws that dictate relationships. Somehow this had not been clear to me in high school. I grew more confident in my interpretations, more sure of where I fit in due to the exegeses I'd performed on the people who surrounded me.

The fallbacks of this approach are so obvious; people are not books. Their sentences are always changing, new chapters added or hastily erased, with the right to change genres or themes at will. To read people otherwise—as though they are static and only your readings can change—is narcissistic. That narcissism is fine with a book, up to a point; no matter how much you understand or misunderstand it, the book won't rewrite itself. (In this sense, a book also won't betray you. It is the only truly secret love affair you can have; the book will never tell what you show it, even as you reveal your truest self to the page.) I learned through trial and error that there were certain people who would never match up with my botched and self-focused interpretations of them. It's not generalizing to say that this kind of deterministic reading was the end of nearly every romantic relationship I undertook in those years, as I was still resolutely seeking my human equivalent of *Possession*, the imagined person I could read thrillingly and completely, down to his bones. I confused love with virtuosic interpretive leaps, with an instinct for reading, with expertise. But even as I learned to be more lenient with my readings of some people through my late teens and twenties, there were others of whom my interpretations only grew more and more concrete and unrevisable.

One of them was my best friend, Becca. As with *Possession*, we had also had a meet-cute, or rather a miss-cute. Early in our relationship, we discovered that not only did we grow up about an hour apart from each other, on opposite sides of the greater Cleveland area, but also by sheer bizarre chance we'd both stayed at the same Berlin youth hostel for a few bitter cold spring days of the last year; she could swear she'd even seen me and my friend bickering in the bar and wisely decided not to approach. Despite these close encounters, we did not meet until several weeks into college. We did not fall in love immediately, unlike my relationship with *Possession*. Instead, we developed that kind of friendship that builds up out of the tiny grains of shared time that are the by-product of school or a certain kind of workplace—the kind of situation where you are often together, underoccupied, and mercifully unhurried.

I'm sorry to say that we met in an a cappella group. Neither of us would have rushed a sorority if our lives depended on it, but we accidentally found ourselves in a cultish version of one anyway, where emotional closeness was oddly conflated with perfect vocal blend. I don't remember how we developed a more particular friendship in that atmosphere of militantly enforced communal intimacy. But for some reason we began to seek each other out before and after rehearsal, discovering over dining hall meals that our alarm clock radios had awakened us to the same radio station all through middle school, we both reread Susan Cooper's *The Dark Is Rising* every year at midwinter, we had both grown up without cable but still somehow had developed a feverish attachment to *Daria* (to this day the only couple's costume I have ever participated in, she as Daria and I as Jane senior year). These small, shared affinities cracked open the door to the real stuff. We were preoccupied with many of the same things but came at them from opposite directions. We both experienced our parents' love as crushing pressure, but she worried she might disappoint hers by not being as happy as they hoped she'd be, while I was certain that I would only disappoint mine if I pursued anything that made me happy. When we met, she avoided thinking about things like clothes and hair with an assiduous dismissal that was as much anxiety as disregard, while I sometimes was unable to go to class because I couldn't put together an outfit that felt exactly right, reduced to tears amid piles of outlandish Salvation Army finds on the floor of my chaotic closet (unsurprisingly, perhaps, we were both later diagnosed with OCD). We could rarely understand each other's choices even if we could almost always guess what they would be. We were nothing alike; we were too alike.

I think we must have been something of an odd couple; people commented on this often, not sure what we saw in each other. I could not have explained it; who can explain love? Over the four years we were in college together, without even realizing it, we started speaking the kind of all-encompassing shorthand idiolect that only the closest relationships—lifelong friends, siblings, partners—develop. By the time we moved to Seattle together after graduation with two other friends, it felt like we knew everything about each other, and yet occasional moments of utter surprise and unforeseen conflict were still possible. Despite this, I thought I understood exactly the parameters of both our friendship and ourselves. We were in our early twenties then, and I was still preoccupied with trying to find the great, dramatic love story of my youth. But perhaps I was just in denial about the fact that we were already living an undramatic, far more meaningful version of it.

The other person who suffered the longest under the strict
rule of my personal textual interpretations was, unsurprisingly, me. Up until college, I'd not had a story to tell about
why I was the way I was. The weeks or months of dull unfeel-
ing and exhaustion, the days in a row when I could not stop
crying at the slightest provocation, the way I couldn't make
myself smile when I was home with both of my parents,
whether my dad cajoled or screamed at me—I'd never had
reasons for these things. It was just life, nonnarrative and inescapable. When I got to college, though, emboldened by my
newfound ability to not just read things well but read *into*
them, I started to sketch out my story, one that I reinforced
and added on to through the years. The story grew and slowly
calcified as the years passed, and I was first convinced and
then stiflingly encased by it. Everyone around me was writing
their own stories, too, either polishing and embellishing old
ones or inventing new ones for themselves out of whole cloth.

And I stuck to mine—while other people tried out new
things and shaped themselves into new people, I dug down
deeper into my established character traits. I knew a lot of
things about myself, and nothing could tell me otherwise. I
knew I was a smoker; I became such a constant fixture on the
bench outside our freshman dorm that when it was carried off
by the dwellers of a neighboring benchless entryway, an indignant crowd of people came to my aid and moved it back. I
knew that my parents were the cause of all my troubles; I had
a backlog of detailed complaints and oft-repeated incident
reports that I had been collecting and would gleefully enu-
merate to any unfortunate friend who found me in the wrong
mood. I knew that A. S. Byatt was my favorite novelist, even
more so because nobody in my classes knew or cared who she

was; I wrote my yearlong senior thesis on the Barthesian pleasure of the text in *Possession*. I also knew that I was a lost
cause, and that eventually I would have to go back to my old
hobby, suicide.

I never sought help because I was so sure that help was not
possible. It was so impossible it was not even thinkable—and
not even desirable. To humor Becca, I did once make an ap-
pointment with a mental health counselor, at the department
that was still hilariously slash alarmingly called "Mental Hy-
giene." The therapist, a gaunt white thirtysomething woman
whose brown bob was as dangerously sharp as her forward-
jutting collarbones, leaned in and asked conspiratorially,
"Don't you think that it's your patriarchal culture that makes
your father act like this?" I never went back, feeling even more
smugly confident that only I could read my own story cor-
rectly. It was perversely pleasurable.

And I also knew in my most abject heart that the only
thing that could save me from my tragic fate was romantic
love, and romantic love looked like reading. I knew that I
needed someone to come along and read me as clearly as I
read myself, as I'd read Byatt that night on the plane, and feel
that reading like "stones of fire, like points of stars in the
dark." Who that reader would be was the only part of my
story that was left temporarily blank. Otherwise, it was all so
definite. I felt sure that I alone could see how the plot of my
own life worked, where I had been and where I was fated to
go. It never occurred to me that Becca was quietly reading me
this whole time, in a workmanlike and scholarly way. This figure of a caring, diligent, loving but unromantic reader didn't
fit into my vision of both literature and life, which was filled
with showy virtuosity and arrogant command. Our friendship

was, from the beginning, structured by two things: my impe-
rious pronouncements that things had to be a certain way and
her generous habit of nodding along and humoring me as far
as was responsible. I didn't see that for all those years she was
unassumingly working away at a competing reading of who
we each were, taking detailed mental notes for her own interpretation of the collaboratively authored text of our friendship, and that perhaps hers was the better and truer one.

*

I was not happy, but the feeling of accomplished expertise
that I derived from poring over my constant, confident self-
analysis gave me something like joy. I was proud of knowing
so much about myself; everyone else, I thought, was so naïve
with their suggestions that I might find a different therapist
or try yoga or deep breathing or whatever. My *Possession* essay
won a prize and my pride at my critical abilities redoubled.
After graduation, I took a couple of years away from school,
but after working a few random jobs with little success, I
glibly disregarded all the digs that Byatt takes at academic life
and decided to pursue the one thing I knew I could do: I went
to graduate school to read novels.

Possession is full of the kinds of academic you don't want to
be. The competitive striving to be the closest to the text, the
greatest expert in it, is exactly what makes for the lonely, solitary figures who populate the novel alongside Roland and
Maud. And there are plenty of examples of the love between
the reader and the reading gone wrong, the love of literature
somehow thwarted or warped. The worst example of this is
the novel's villain, the ominously named Mortimer Cropper

(whose Americanness is also, in this very English novel, extremely ominous). Cropper, the scion of a wealthy family who works at a wealthy university in New Mexico, loves Randolph Ash with a morbid possessiveness, and his fetishism of the dead man has a necrophiliac quality; there is nothing good or life-giving about the way that he acts out his desire to possess the poet for himself.

But to counter the moneyed machinations of Cropper—whose very name summons up the image of the Grim Reaper—the lively, loving bliss of reading is thematized in the two pairs of lovers. This is what I was sure I would be able to hold on to in graduate school. We often witness Maud and Roland reading, together and apart, and in these moments, we begin to see the inexorability of their attraction. Unlike their colleagues, they both retain a kind of miraculously untarnished passion for the objects of their study; as Maud says, they both work on what they work on not *because* they have studied it for so long, but rather, in spite of that fact: For her, Christabel, and for him, Ash, remain so important in a real, emotional as well as intellectual way because they are "what could survive our education." And the texts that they work on are, in their hands alone, somehow alive.

And indeed, some of graduate school *was* like that. I found so many more texts to fall disastrously, extravagantly in love with, in ways that offered variations on the experience I'd had with Byatt all those years ago. But at the same time, there suddenly seemed to be consequences to reading indiscriminately. It seemed that my reading, and my writing about reading, was often irresponsible, by which my professors and peers meant that it was undertheorized, uninformed, and unresearched. This was a brutal lesson that I came to appreciate.

I continued to read passionately and often with a dash of my old haphazardness but developed parameters of thought and rigor that shaped how I read and channeled even the most randomly stumbled-upon texts into my dissertation's over-arching argument. And so, I became accustomed to, even dependent upon, a kind of disciplined liberty, one in which more and more, I sought out books that I could account for conscientiously in my writing, even if—or especially when—they were difficult or challenging. I became a professional reader. I accepted that, while objectivity was impossible, subjectivity was perhaps avoidable.

*

I applied the same defensive certainty and faux-scientific professionalized self-confidence to my avid readings of myself and the people around me. I was in two long relationships through grad school, but looking back, they didn't stand a chance. I was too determined a reader of who I was and what I needed, and my arguments for the decisions I made were often completely misled.

Boyfriends came and went. The person who stayed in my life solidly this whole time, not subject to the demand for bombast or epiphany, was Becca. We shared many of the most important late-early-life moments, like the cathartic night when she decided she finally had to leave her first, worst boy-friend who was jealously holding her back, or the blazing hot afternoon on a Williamsburg sidewalk when she patiently stood witness to a terrible two-hour phone argument with my mom that ended with a yearlong separation. But while I recognized their significance, I took for granted the fact that we shared these episodes of destruction and growth and worked them seamlessly into the old narrative structure of our lives together. We lived far apart for years—she moved between New York and Seattle and then Beijing, while I was in the abstract reaches of graduate school, located physically in Berkeley, before my academic job took me to New York—but I always assumed that I knew what was happening with her, and she with me. Eventually we both ended up in Brooklyn, where we contentiously shared an apartment for the first time in nearly ten years.

Over the course of our friendship, I came to think of myself as the world's foremost Becca expert. There was a possessiveness to how I treated our friendship. It wasn't that I needed to be Becca's only friend, but I needed to believe myself the most knowledgeable one. Even as my other relationships were shifting and changing, by dint of the age and accustomed intensity of it, my friendship with Becca remained static. I was still holding on to the notion that one could have complete knowledge of someone else. But *Becca* was not static, even if my conception of our relationship, or even if I, was. I see now that she was shockingly patient and forgiving of me for years, as I bossed her around and thought I knew her better than she knew herself. Our friendship continued to survive the structure I imposed on it only because she was willing to distort herself to keep fitting the cramped space I gave her when we were together.

The wrongness of this was hidden, in plain sight, in *Possession*. Believing that it is his right to know about and to own everything belonging to the poets he's become an expert in, Mortimer Cropper uses that exact same language. Determined to plunder an actual grave to get to the bottom

of the mystery of Ash and LaMotte, he chillingly declares
that he will do whatever it takes to learn what the poets
"concealed from us. *I intend to know.*" I had, over the course
of our relationship and many others that did not survive,
become Cropper.

It took me many successive relationship failures to acknowledge this fact. I first saw it in romance. While my interest in building stories with and around other people made me
very good at starting relationships, it was not as good at sus-
taining them. The next received narrative to fall apart was my
understanding of myself as an expert reader. I made it through
grad school by reading idiosyncratically, priding myself on
making and defending odd interpretive choices simply because they tickled me, refusing to subscribe to any single
methodology. I was completely confident in my ability to in-
vent my way through a text, and I think it was largely that
confidence that, to everyone's surprise, got me a job. Once I
started that job, though, creative bravado was not enough. As
it seemed more and more important to be an expert, I felt less
and less like one; my readings again were accused of being
undertheorized, uninformed, unresearched, and now unpro-
fessional. That Cropper-like possessive arrogance fell away as
did my confidence in my ability to read that had been building ever since reading *Possession* on that fateful flight so many
years before. After a few years, I no longer felt safe calling
myself a professional reader, and, more alarmingly, I sometimes had difficulty feeling like any kind of reader at all. I
didn't feel like I'd fallen out of love with books, but I did feel
uneasily like they'd fallen out of love with me.

For whatever reason, the last reading that I held on to with
that old arrogant certainty was my reading of Becca. Perhaps

it is because she enabled me, seeing what a toll these other losses were taking on my mental well-being. Or perhaps it is because I knew intuitively and subconsciously that this was real love, and real love would survive for longer than it should, even when it's mistreated and taken for granted. Even after my breakdown, when I had let go of everything else I was sure about, I held on to my belief in how our friendship worked, assuming I knew everything we could offer each other. This supposed knowledge was ultimately the thing that drove a wedge between us—invisibly at first, then with an awkward and increasingly painful obviousness. After being together through the pandemic—she was one of the few people in my pod—I felt wearily afraid that we knew each other so well that it was the end of knowing.

When lockdown loosened up—I'm not proud of this—we barely spoke for months. I felt certain I knew how every conversation we could ever have would go. It was not fair, not fair at all. I'd been treating her like a book I'd read and read and then outgrown, not realizing that if I went back and read closely, the words meant something different after all those years. When eventually we met to hash out what had happened in our months of separation, I realized that in the last many years, Becca's text had been changing—perhaps not the words that sketched out her character, but their tone, their meaning. She had been reading me sensitively all the while. She was concerned and attuned to the interpretive shifts in the text of my life, but I had not been looking at her with the same openness and generosity. I thought belatedly about how many other people and things I'd been regarding in the same inflexible way for so long.

Certainly, *Possession* was one of those things. Once I began
to reread my friendship with Becca, I looked back at the novel,
which I've known for just slightly longer than I've known her.
For the first time in a few years, I reread it—*really* reread it
cover to cover, not just dipping in and out to revisit sections
or find references. It was, I was shocked to find, both a different book and exactly the same one. Lines that I knew almost
by heart resonated differently; perhaps it was my heart that
had changed. After being jostled down the assembly line of
academia and falling off the conveyor belt at the other end,
Roland's moment of epiphany was even more powerful than I
remembered. I found myself wondering, for the very first
time, what happened after the end of the novel. Roland finally
receives multiple offers for academic positions he's been ap-
plying to for years, and in the past, I assumed that he would
take one of them. This time, though, I contemplated the
dawning understanding that astonished both Roland and me
so much: "He had time to feel the strangeness of before and
after; an hour ago there had been no poems, and now they
came like rain and were real." As I reread these words, the
poems felt so much more real than all the predetermined
readings I imagined him delivering from the lectern as an
academic. Even though Roland is an imaginary character and
I myself had been reading the book off and on for more than
twenty years, I felt an eager new hope leap up, that he would
say no to those jobs and stay with Maud and become a poet. I
was shocked: I had thought that I knew everything there was
to know about it, but somehow the book still held surprises.

Possession reminds us constantly that what we love must be
allowed to retain its little secrets. It enacts this, most notably,

in its epilogue, that last page that my teacher found so sad (and which does, in fact, grow sadder to me the older I get). But there's also a flirtatious assertion of dominance that the narrator occasionally exercises the further we get into the book. The closer we get to narrative resolution, the more play-fully convoluted it becomes. *You may think you're in control,* the book says, *but* I'll *tell you what you want and what you can have, and when you can have it.* It doesn't let its reader forget that any text, and any person, too, has its right to tell or not to tell, to surprise us when it can, to always be open to changeable meanings and interpretations even as its words remain—wonderfully—immutably the same.

Chapter 5

PEERING

In the last week of June 2018, I got unexpectedly dumped. During the month that followed, I did the only thing that felt right: I read Anne Carson's long poem "The Glass Essay" every day. I had gone to Oxford to teach a summer class as England endured a historic drought, and the sun shone heartlessly, beautifully every day. Every morning, I woke up, ran around the park, rushed through a shower and a coffee, and ascended to the upper reading room of the Radcliffe Camera, one of Oxford's extravagantly beautiful libraries. I would claim my favorite desk, with my favorite graffito ("LIBIDINAL COMMUNISM") etched in its wood frame, and lean back in my chair, staring up into the rotunda's scrolled dome. Then, once my mind was blank and still, usually around 9:25, I'd open Carson and begin. The poem starts:

> I can hear little clicks inside my dream.
> Night drips its silver tap

down the back.
At 4 A.M. I wake. Thinking

of the man who
left in September.
His name was Law.

From the first time I read them after the breakup, these
lines laced me into the poem good and tight. "The Glass
Essay" is a complex structure, holding two disparate elements
together in a surprising balance: an intimate meditation on a
romantic breakup, and a critical reading of the life of Emily
Brontë. The poem immediately became the frame I required
to shape the posture of my hours; I needed to read it to stay
upright during the day and to stay lying down at night. I too
know that slow, cold drip down the spine because I'm a bad
sleeper; at 4:00 A.M. I'm always either going to bed or suddenly starting awake. But the main point of identification
was so obvious I didn't even bother to note it: I was going
through a breakup, and "The Glass Essay" is indisputably the
greatest breakup poem ever written. (Don't try to argue with
me on this.) The urge to reread flowed out of my desire to
sink further into the poem and its speaker and remain there,
a desire that in turn flowed out of the deeper, inane desire
(Carson's, my own) to sink further into the memory of the
departed lover and remain *there*. On the cusp of dark and
dawn, I would lie in my narrow bed and try to memorize the
whole thirty-eight-page poem. I never got very far, but certain lines snagged in my mind. The moments that really cut
were where the language is plainest, most painful: "His name
was Law."

This yearning for a lost lover named Law raises a question: Is to be loveless to be lawless? If Law equals love, then is love—when requited, respected—the thing that keeps us in line, restrained and civil? Certainly, both loss and longing are states of emergency, outside the law. Perhaps to be with Law is to be governed by him, or by desire for him. Or is it the opposite? One brief moment in the poem seems like it might offer an answer, but then flatly refuses to:

> Well, there are different definitions of Liberty.
> Love is freedom, Law was fond of saying.
> I took this to be more a wish than a thought
>
> and changed the subject.

The man who fractured my heart that summer, and cleanly broke it later on, was also fond of speculating about love and freedom. For someone who talked and wrote a lot to friends and strangers, he didn't put much stake in the verbal as a mode of emotional honesty. Looking back, I wonder now if he thought love was the freedom not to explain yourself, a millennial version of Ali MacGraw's catchphrase in *Love Story:* "Love means never having to say you're sorry." Love, to him, was something like a complete freedom of self-expression so expansive and natural it didn't have to be contained in words but could instead be communicated purely through gaze, or touch, or atmospheric resonance. I believe in gazes and touches and atmospheres, but I cannot—and would never—forsake my belief in words. I am most free and real when jostling around restlessly in the human laboratory of dialogue.

But dialogue requires someone who will talk back: That is its fundamental rule. It is proof of the lawlessness of love that I could love him when we didn't even agree that this rule existed.

*

His name was Luck.

Luck because I met him at a time when I was stoutly resisting the temptation to declare myself terminally unlucky in love. I did not want to let myself off the hook like that, did not want to make lame cosmic excuses for my loneliness with abstractions like fate or doom. But then I met him and knew that luck was real, because he just appeared one day, out of the ether of a dating app. We found that we craved the same foods, laughed at the same small things, liked the same smells and colors. It was plain good fortune to have met. In fact, it was the first major stroke of fortune I'd had since I started the teaching job in which I had been flailing—unfit and unwell, rather than unlucky—for several years. And now here was Luck, another outwardly successful person who had his own share of doubts and regrets and empathized with my feeling of unfitness and unease. We were both sad, lucky people who felt that our luck was unearned, a problem that is understandably very annoying to most. What luck to have found each other!

When Luck left me that June, I gave in to the mortifying feeling that I was loveless, outside the laws of normal life. The months in England were a mourning time, I told myself with false confidence. When I went home in the fall, it would be over—not better, just *over*. And so I sank and took "The Glass Essay" down with me, not yet understanding that it had much more to teach me about than the loss of love.

*

I hadn't intended to read "The Glass Essay" at all, as I'd never considered myself a responsible reader of Anne Carson. Since I was not a classicist, and her work is suffused with classical references and texts, I felt I would not have permission until I learned enough about the ancient poets to read her properly— and so, realistically, never. But a couplet from "The Glass Essay" I had seen quoted in a friend's dissertation stuck in my mind:

> When Law left I felt so bad I thought
>   I would die.
> This is not uncommon.

When Luck left me, these lines resurfaced. That's it, I thought. That is love. The blank honesty of the couplet made me need Carson; I had to give in to her.

In Oxford, I was supposed to be writing the scholarly book I never finished; instead, I summoned up a short stack of Carson from the depths of the Bodleian. Slim books with great, epic names: *Glass, Irony & God; Eros the Bittersweet; Economy of the Unlost*. I encountered "The Glass Essay" upon opening the first of these. For a few days it was just something I was muddling through, a poem I was still in the midst of deciphering. But by the end of that week, I had read it and annotated it and read it again, and I still felt a need for it. I could not read anything else until I had satisfied that need. "The Glass Essay" stood in the way of any other text. That's how it became part of my daily schedule: run, shower, coffee, read "The Glass Essay," work. On the weekends, when the reading room was closed and LIBIDINAL COMMUNISM inaccessible, I'd change it up a little: read "The Glass Essay" upon waking, run, coffee, shower, work. As someone who thinks mostly about novels, I am shy around poetry; I feel often as though it is reading me more than I am reading it. After years of feeling that way, it was strange to wake up and read a poem every day, and to feel I had grown intimate with it, tender with its idiosyncrasies of form and rhythm. For four or five weeks this went on, the poem becoming as falsely natural as a piercing, a foreign body fitted snugly into the internal and external material of my life.

To make clear the strangeness of this, I must first admit to being a compulsive failed self-improver. My parents hoped to attain eternal life through dietary restriction; trained from childhood to respect other people's regimens, I've always admired those who can develop systems of personal organization and live consistently within them. Perhaps in reaction to the strictness of my childhood, I am not one of those people. At the beginning of every school year, I make detailed schedules for days of teaching, days of writing, days of reading, but after a week or two, everything falls apart, and the only plans I can follow are my lesson plans. I am addicted to working and thinking as the spirit moves me, in the maddening way that only the unattached, often depressive person can get away with: seventy-two-hour writing benders, followed by days or weeks of melancholic collapse; periods of mental slog punctuated by a sudden sprint through five or six books without breaks for food or movement. I recognize the decadence of this lifestyle. In the brief neutral moments between these altered states, I find it extremely embarrassing and self-indulgent. Yet no matter how many rules I attempt to impose upon myself, the only predictable cycle I maintain is the endless loop of plans made, plans broken, self-flagellation.

So, the Carson program came as a real surprise. The closest experience I'd had to it were the days, governed by animal schedules, that I'd spent working on farms during summer breaks on and off throughout my life. In fact, there was something reassuringly animal-like about the predetermined hours of that month, as though the poem were the morning scoop of grain I needed to ruminate on to give me enough energy to move through the day. The poem was necessary sustenance.

*

In staring at Carson's words day after day, I found myself doing something I almost never did, and had been trained in graduate school not to be tempted by: I started to see myself reflected in them. I fell deeply and unquestioningly into identification with the speaker, seeking out similarities, imagining that we felt the same emotions and sensations. It was like falling in love.

The line "Mother and I are chewing lettuce carefully" brought back the diet-ruled dinners of my childhood, my parents and I silently chewing cold leaves and roots with grim concentration. The speaker doesn't like to lie late in bed in the mornings, and neither do I. Soon I even felt a tug of fond

familiarity reading about things that I don't do or feel. Standing at the open refrigerator, the speaker says,

> White foods taste best to me
> and I prefer to eat alone. I don't know why.

    I don't feel any particular way about white foods, and I pre-
fer to eat in company. But rereading those lines, I was mo-
mentarily certain that I too felt as the speaker did and had to
remind myself that this was not the case. These tiny, domestic
sympathies, embedded in a poem that deals with the very biggest questions—What is love? What is God? What is art,
who dares attempt it, and at what cost? What are mother and
father and self?—folded me into the text with a bodily im-
mediacy, rather than keeping me at the cool distance of scholarly reading.

    Looking back, I wonder if cultivating intimacy with the
text in this way was a self-soothing mechanism. I don't think
it was. Processing the breakup through this act of rereading,
redoubling, and remembering revolved around the neutral
cruelty of repetition. Having "The Glass Essay" on a loop
made everything feel like the present, not the past. As Carson
writes,

> Perhaps the hardest thing about losing a lover is
> to watch the year repeat its days.
> It is as if I could dip my hand down
>
> into time and scoop up
> blue and green lozenges of April heat
> a year ago in another country.

I can feel that other day running underneath
        this one
    like an old videotape . . .

After you walk away from a last goodbye, the terrain of
everyday life is suddenly overlaid with the haunted geography
of an entire relationship. Every space is layered with the fine
sediment of recollection. Any time you trip and reach out for
balance, your hand might accidentally slip "down // into time"
and dredge up something beautiful or awful from those years
or months or weeks past.

The self, too, is multiplied, and might cross itself if you are
not careful. As time slides and aligns and blurs, so too does
Carson's speaker feel her present self slip into a past self of the
hot last April, inhabiting simultaneously a then-"she," trapped
in memory, and a now-"I," writing in the present. Typing
these lines, even now I feel my heartbeat echo itself for a moment with syncopated desire. I feel the chilly presence of my
own ghostly double from this time that year; she is sitting at
this same desk, awaiting Luck's response to a long email of
supplication, nauseated by the mingling of hope and exhaustion.

All the moments with Luck were there at once, and all the
selves that I had been in relation to him, too. The self reading
Carson in the library; the self lying on my floor a few weeks
earlier, asking him what he thought love was; the self dashing
around cooking dinner with him in his tiny kitchen. *Il punto
a cui tutti li tempi son presenti,* to crib Dante's mystical phrase:
"the point when all the times are present." The ritualized rereading of "The Glass Essay" summoned all these times and
held them in shimmering alignment, just as Carson's speaker

feels moments overlapping in the poem. I wonder if a part of me still believed, childishly, that the repeated incantation of a name or a phrase is a powerful summoning spell—you know, "Bloody Mary, Bloody Mary, Bloody Mary," "Beetlejuice, Beetlejuice, Beetlejuice." (Luck, Luck, Luck.) Could the repeated reading of a poem bring its words into my actual life in a consequential way? In those weeks, I did feel something uncanny was coming over me and Oxford, which was bleached unfamiliar shades of straw and gold by the drought. I couldn't tell if this was an effect of the text or of my compulsive rereading of it.

Of course, Carson's poem enacts a similar question: It is itself a lyric essay on rereading Emily Brontë, and how this rereading leads the speaker to view the conditions of her life differently. When it opens, the speaker has retreated to her mother's house in the remote North to convalesce from the loss of Law. She takes with her:

> . . . a lot of books—
>
> some for my mother, some for me
> including *The Collected Works Of Emily Brontë*.
> This is my favourite author.

We find "three silent women at the kitchen table": Carson, her mother, and Emily, communicating blurrily as through an "atmosphere of glass." The odd presence of Emily at that kitchen table, quietly lurking inside her book, made me think about the presence of Anne Carson in my own day-to-day activities, an Anne Carson I began to half imagine as embodied rather than em-booked. Anne Carson jogging lightly beside me in the park, Anne Carson absentmindedly humming behind me in the coffee queue, Anne Carson sitting opposite me in the library, leaning back coolly in her chair like a rebel in a high school movie, watching me read her poem for the thirteenth or twenty-third time.

This strange feeling of possession was itself mimetic of the poem. For just as I felt myself inhabiting Carson's "I," so does Carson's speaker feel herself doubling her "favourite author." Yet Emily, writes Carson, is also

> ... my main fear, which I mean to confront.
> Whenever I visit my mother
> I feel I am turning into Emily Brontë,
>
> my lonely life around me like a moor,
> my ungainly body stumping over the mud flats
>   with a look of transformation
> that dies when I come in the kitchen door.

All the things I was warned away from as a professional student of literature—not to confuse the poet with the speaker, not to get mired in biography, not to be fooled by the cheap lure of identification—went out the window as this possession overcame us. We were three silent women, moving through the pages of books and years. Carson peered into Brontë's poems as I peered into her own poem, looking for—something.

*

Luck was always trying to plumb my depths, in a manner I found both sweet and offensive. He always wanted more and wouldn't believe me when I said I'd told him everything. When eventually he saw that I really had given him everything I knew about myself, he found the offering wanting. It was only a few weeks into our relationship, when I first experienced the well-intentioned ferocity of his desire to understand me better than I understood myself. He wasn't really a drinker, but he poured us both a scotch and alternatingly interrogated and flirted with me. I was attracted and confused. Here was someone who wanted to know more about me, but his playful manner of asking very serious questions made his desire seem like part of a game. Did he really want to see me, or did he simply want to be allowed to see *something*, to be granted the pleasure of mere access?

The idea of seeing, *really* seeing, was more important to him than it was to anyone I'd ever known. On our second or third date, he casually told me that he was face-blind—a condition I'd never heard of. He was, as he said, "bad at faces." This was a self-deprecating understatement. It would take him, he estimated, twenty or thirty meetings with someone to be able to recognize that person's face. If I put my hair up or let it down, took my glasses off or put them on, he suddenly saw me as a stranger. This explained, I thought, the way he'd pause and examine my face every time we met, a smile playing around his lips, looking for the person he was coming to know. The longer we were together, the more his face blindness confused me: How much did he recognize me? How much did it matter if he didn't or couldn't ever? I came to terms with this, telling myself that at the very least, I would always know if he found me attractive. My fear was that one day, out of the blue, he wouldn't. It worried me—and in some way I'll never understand, I'm sure it worried him, too.

Thinking about him now, I have to stop myself from narrative reduction, the cruelest thing I could do to a person I still care about. Luck is not just a character in my story; he has his own. It's too easy to draw a neat, simplistic parallel: Luck felt he never recognized me emotionally because his brain couldn't recognize me physically. That's not it, though. Looking back, I begin to understand that he was also peering into me in the hope that he would find a mirror that could show him his truest self, that would instructively reveal what he looked like in love. I don't say this with resentment but rather with what remains of love. Another kind of compulsive rereading, you might say. To look into the person you're with over and over again, telling yourself that you're trying to comprehend them more fully, can simply be a means of understanding your own reading self. This self that reads other people is not the same as the self that might read a poem—but it is not entirely different. It had taken me so many years to realize this about myself and even so, it would take two more years to see this in Luck. I grew tired of being peered at and tired of trying to see through the thick, impenetrable glass of his own surface.

*

The metaphor is so obvious I barely need to articulate it. Luck peered into me to see himself, then I peered into Carson to see myself, as she peered into Brontë in turn—a nested series of readings and rereadings in the search for newer, deeper meanings. I didn't realize I was doing it at the time; my immersion in Carson's poem was so total that I couldn't take even a step back. I only started to perceive these twinned phenomena somewhere around week three of the Carson regimen.

For Carson, the intense peering activates a powerful, frightening mode of self-reflection, wherein she seems to see right through the illusory exterior of emotion into somewhere more profound and, eventually, more generative. She supplements her reading with periods of rhapsodic meditation, in which a series of twelve female "Nudes" appears to her, visions that she understands to be "a nude glimpse of [her] lone soul, / not the complex mysteries of love and hate." The Nudes are primitively symbolic, tarot-like, their imagery at once hotly interior and coldly objectified. They are violent: a woman's body in agony, flesh ripped away, or pierced by thorns, or stitched by a giant silver needle. They infiltrate me as profoundly as the poem's images of passion. They summon up familiar visions I'd long held at bay: flashbacks to fantasies of my body rendered down, sliced or melted away, accompanied by the scent of self-harm's alchemical compound of desire and terror.

In Emily's poetry (Carson writes), she "had a relationship . . . with someone she calls Thou," who may be God or Death, or something undefined. Emily, in her apparent isolation, seems to have had a clearer understanding than I of how to relate to the other, even if her other is a force, not a person. It seems strange to turn for advice on love to Emily Brontë, a woman who was "unable to meet the eyes of strangers when she ventured out," and according to her biographers led a "sad, stunted life . . . Uninteresting, unremarkable, wracked by disappointment / and despair." Yet it is through Brontë that

Carson—and through Carson, I—begin to really ask the fundamental questions: How are we to look at a loved one, and
how are we to look at ourselves? Weird Emily, communing
intermittently with Thou, might offer some kind of better answer than what I'd gleaned from human relationships for how
to be held closely yet at a distance, in some state of perpetual
transit between the "inside outside" and the "outside inside."
"Thou and Emily influence one another in the darkness,"
writes Carson, "playing near and far at once." Something
about this seeming paradox of location, near and far, inside
and outside, and the way that Emily flits between the two,
seems to hold some promise of escaping the mere self. Her
word for this is "whaching":

> Whacher,
> Emily's habitual spelling of this word,
> has caused confusion.
> . . . .
> Whacher is what she was.
> She whached God and humans and moor wind
>   and open night.
> She whached eyes, stars, inside, outside, actual
>   weather.
>
> She whached the bars of time, which broke.
> She whached the poor core of the world,
> wide open.

   Whaching is not simply watching; while Emily whached
things we can all observe, like "humans" and "actual weather,"

she also whached those things that cannot be witnessed, like "God" and "the poor core of the world." Whaching is seeing beyond mere physical vision, knowing beyond determined thought. It allows her to be at once inside and outside of herself; by whaching, Emily breaks "the bars of time" and seems to exist outside its prison. Somehow whaching is less an action than a state of being:

> To be a Whacher is not a choice.
> There is nowhere to get away from it
> . . . .
> To be a Whacher is not in itself sad or happy.

To whach is a calling. If Emily is a Whacher, then so too is Carson by the end of the poem—but only after she stops trying so hard to *watch,* to "peer and glance," seeking symbolic meaning or resolution, seeking to solve the problem of herself with and without Law. After the period of rereading Brontë, staring into herself, and seeing the Nudes, the whole thing simply stops:

> I stopped watching.
> I forgot about Nudes.
> I lived my life,

> which felt like a switched-off TV.
> Something had gone through me and out and
>   I could not own it.

At first, this moment feels deflating, emptied of the exhilaration of what she earlier calls her "spiritual melodrama" and intense feeling. But then something amazing happens. The poem ends with a final vision, a thirteenth Nude. Though it resembles the first Nude—the woman standing naked and bloody on a hill, strips of flesh flayed by the wind—this figure is not in pain. It stands, neutral and unflinching,

> . . . a human body

> trying to stand against winds so terrible that the
>   flesh was blowing off the bones.
> And there was no pain.
> The wind
> was cleansing the bones.
> They stood forth silver and necessary.
> It was not my body, not a woman's body, it was the
>   body of us all.
> It walked out of the light.

On one of the late Carson days, maybe Tuesday or Wednesday of the fourth week, this moment gave me a new shock. And it led me to consider my own spiritual melodrama, and my ways of peering and rereading. All that bloody revealing, that squinting and seeking, hadn't gotten down to the bones of the situation. It didn't open up the poor core of my world or any other; it only abandoned me in the foggy region between past and present, my vision clouded by layers of feeling. I was not whaching right, and I knew it. But I was learning.

Learning to whach meant getting both closer to and further away from my deep identification with the poem's speaker. The closer I got to the poem as a whole, the further I got from myself; the further I got from the self, the more clearly could I see it. Thinking of what it means to whach, I am tempted now just to call it really "reading"—reading as it might be wholly integrated into lived experience.

In that month of rereading, I was peering at "The Glass Essay" so intently for my own reflection, trying to scry through it my own feelings, the resolution of my own sadness. But once those feelings were gone, I could look at the poem and the breakup directly, through the transparent pane of that old reading. I could see that old self, and the poem, and the loss of Luck more lucidly than before. I was not looking for myself in Carson's reading of Brontë, or in Carson's Nudes, or in Carson's breakup story. I was not looking for anything anymore.

*

Or perhaps it's more honest to say that I was looking for nothing.

I did eventually learn something real about whaching from "The Glass Essay"—I haven't lied to you. But that took another few years of rereading the poem even more, writing and rewriting this book, thinking and rethinking that time. What happened next, back in 2018, was less inspirational, and less neatly resolved. It's very rare that stories just unfold in neat, storified form. I did get a temporary measure of peace out of the Carson routine, and for the last week of my stay in England, I felt a sudden calm—so sudden and so calm I should have identified it as foreboding. Merve and her family moved to Oxford just as I was getting ready to leave it, and it was easy to spend time with them, sitting in the garden and listen-

ing to speculations about what their new life in this old country would be like. For the first time in a long while, I felt
dreamily removed from my own life. This calm lent me the
sensation of great smugness, another clear sign that I had not,
in fact, attained enlightenment through sustained close reading. In the moment, though, I told myself firmly that I had
figured something out: how to look *at* nothing, how to look
for nothing. How to feel nothing, which I mistook for the
ideal state of being. How to feel *like* nothing, which, at the
time, I believed was the only reasonable position.

I thought this was wisdom. Now, I see it was self-defense.
Worse, it was a self-defense tactic that I'd unconsciously employed many times in the past, in the lulls between depressive
episodes. It was a way of abdicating selfhood, dispersing myself willfully into a kind of mist that spread thinly across the
landscape of my life, almost invisible to anyone, the way I
imagined myself disappearing into Anne's Avonlea when I
was young. Almost invisible to myself. As in the month of
Carson, these periods of non-depression were often periods
of intense reading. Countering my episodes of deep immersion in melancholia with deep immersion in texts was a kind
of balancing mechanism.

For most of my life, I believed that this atomized, powerfully
powerless tranquility was the ideal state. In Oxford, I attrib-
uted it to "The Glass Essay" and to Carson, not yet understanding that I was still reading the poem badly. The peace that
she finds at the end of the poem is fundamentally different
from the almost-pleasant, self-annihilating torpor at which I'd
arrived and for which I felt absurdly, reductively grateful. I had
been sad about the breakup—a focused, contained sadness,

a decoy for everything else that was unraveling—and a special poem had come along that let me read that sadness away. But my belief that this little episode, with its neat beginning and ending, could change the inevitable course of things was desperate wish fulfillment. Looking at it from far away now, it all seems so—well. So transparent.

Chapter 6

A TALE FOR
THE NONBEING

Imagine the book that solves all your problems.

It knows where you come from and where you hope you're going. It reads you as you read it. It observes all your obsessions and neuroses and responds to them, thoughtfully working your secret idiosyncrasies into its plot, its characters, its structures. It knows you like nobody else. It must care for you very deeply. You come to suspect that it might even love you—something you're sure it's trying to tell you, coyly unfolding its secret across blushing pages.

This book might be your companion for a week or a lifetime. Sometimes you commit to it long term; it goes with you everywhere, always. Sometimes it's like one of those feverish friendships that only last a season, a flaring up of feeling that feels like an affair in its urgency and hotness but burns out as suddenly as the conflagration began, leaving you a little pile of ash for an indeterminate period. It helps you understand your life, your self. It gives you a way into an inwardness you had not been able to access before. It could be a mystical twin or lover: Nobody can understand you like this book, and nobody can understand it like you.

Sometimes people make the mistake of believing that this means they are in an intense relationship with the author of said book. The author has nothing to do with it; you do not know each other in any way. If anything, the author is an inconvenience, an extraneous spouse/parent/busybody who needs to be divorced or knocked off because they keep trying to come between you and the book. But nothing can stop the force of your attraction, for however long it lasts. You were meant to be together.

This is the book of your life.

This is the book of your death.

*

Ruth Ozeki's third novel, *A Tale for the Time Being*, was published in March 2013, and it was the first book I bought with my brand-new assistant professor's salary that July, the week I moved into my apartment in New Jersey. It never would have occurred to me to buy a new, full-price hardcover before; I remember how extravagant it felt to carry it out of the unfamiliar local bookstore, its corners as fresh and crisp as its bright colors. It was the first book I put on the built-in shelf in my oddly shaped, very white apartment, furnished only with my first unused couch and my first new mattress and box spring. There was nothing else in the apartment, but its atmosphere vibrated with the discomfiting novelty of owning things. This sensation made me feel very young and dispiritingly old at the same time. I'd arrived there with my boyfriend and the cat from Oakland, the cat wailing operatically in his carrier after his first and last airplane flight, and my parents drove in from Ohio to scoop us up from the Newark airport. When we arrived at the university-owned apartment building, there were several other freshly minted faculty members being dropped off by parents, unloading giant bags from Bed Bath & Beyond and flat-pack IKEA boxes. It was dreadfully like the first day of college, but all of us were elderly freshmen, thirtyish and myopic, with lower back pain and carpal tunnel from typing nonstop through the last half decade of our lives.

I didn't read *A Tale for the Time Being* right away, though. There were too many things to do: a syllabus to plan, a cross-country relationship to blow up, and a hundred pages of my dissertation left to write in order to keep the job I'd just gotten. When I did finally get to it that winter break, in a brief respite between filing my dissertation at Berkeley and filing my first semester of grades at Princeton, I was sleep-deprived and skittishly overwrought by the huge changes that had swept through the last few months—perfectly primed to have my mind blown by a big, pleasingly complex novel.

Ozeki delivered in many unexpected ways. The most surprising of them was how its time-traveling narrative snatched me back through my own past, to a moment I had not thought about for at least a decade. The only conversation I ever had with my father's mother was brief and sad. Looking around the small parlor in the family home in Kagoshima, on a visit that was both first and last, I was caught by the photographs on the family shrine: my great-grandparents, I guessed, and a few aunts and uncles I didn't know about. Old people. But there was one large portrait, at the center, that glowed with sunlight and life, despite the softening grays of its black-and-white finish. It was of a beautiful young man with warm eyes gazing dreamily stage right. He wore an aviator's cap with goggles on top and a jaunty white scarf tucked around his throat. I was fifteen, and he didn't look much older than me. A pyramid of oranges and a tall glass of water sat in front of the frame. I asked my mother who it was, and she, in her halting Japanese, asked my grandmother. It was her younger brother, relayed my mom, who died in the war. His plane was on fire, and he could never get out. Every day she gave him cool water because he was so thirsty—every day, still, after all those decades. As she spoke, my grandmother cried a little, but in an unembarrassed, matter-of-fact way.

I don't know what happened to that picture when she died. A bitter family fight broke out over who would get the house, and I've never been back. After he left Japan, my father was estranged from his parents for thirty years. Now they're gone, but a new feud has seamlessly taken the place of the old; nothing has really changed.

I asked my dad once about his mother's side of the family, not long after that trip, but his face shuttered and he said he thought all the records were destroyed in Nagasaki, where his mother was from. Nagasaki: There were no questions that could be asked once that name was uttered. We had gone there when we were in Japan, but he'd been blandly, suspiciously even-tempered as we walked around the city after visiting the Atomic Bomb Museum, chattering instead about castella cake and sixteenth-century Christian martyrs and *Madame Butterfly*. My dad was a shameless liar and an avid fabulist, but I think at least what he said about my grandmother's family was true, or at least he believed it to be so. And that was the end of it: It was a given that most questions asked of him didn't get answered. Even now, I don't know the basic facts of my father's life, like what year he came to the States, when he went to Canada, or why; I don't even think my mother knows for sure. All I know from the few true or false bones my father would occasionally toss us is that his father's family was a military one, going back to samurai roots in Satsuma. There are occasional references in naval histories that seem to confirm this claim. My dad seemed to be proud of this heritage in a conflicted way. He loved to talk up his family's aristocratic connections—a pair of cuff links bearing a family crest that incorporated the royal chrysanthemum occasionally appeared and disappeared in a flash—but definitive proof of this was never offered. He was a terrible snob about how my mother's family ("Peasants!") were dark-skinned fishermen from the backwater of Tottori and made it clear that it was only *his* family and traditions that mattered to us. But at the same time, he had the love-hate relationship to Japan that so many immigrants do to their homelands; despite the fact that he worked for a Japanese company and frequently returned, the Japan that he would wax alternately lyrical and bitter about was frozen in the mid-sixties, whenever he'd left that first time. The wound of his break with his parents didn't heal, even when it was patched up briefly before my grandfather's death, and he never wanted to talk about the generations that came before him and his brothers. My father himself was born in 1944 somewhere in what I assume was Japanese-occupied China, the only date in his life before my parents' marriage that has ever been confirmed; I saw his passport once.

That date, in that place, asks so many unanswerable questions. I've wondered many times if that's why my dad didn't want to talk about the past. I've been told that my grandfather opposed the war; he and my grandmother both worked for the Red Cross, he as a doctor and she as a nurse. But nobody else was ever mentioned. I am afraid to find out how other long-dead, distant relatives in that military family might have participated in the perpetration of violence in China, or in any other sites of Japanese imperial oppression. I have always carried a passive guilt about being Japanese in America rather than Japanese American. This guilt sits separate from the toxic slurry of feelings I have for what Viet Thanh Nguyen calls "America ™," and the crimes this country has committed against Japanese Americans or against my own relatives in Nagasaki or Hiroshima. This is a guilt that pulls me across the ocean, across time. Unlike Ruth Ozeki's mother, or my mother's Canadian cousins that we were never encouraged to know, my father's family were not interned; my ancestors fought for Japan in more than one bloody Pacific war. Because of this I often have the nagging feeling that I don't have a right to belong to an Asian American community. Instead, I nervously anticipate that the Korean, Chinese, Taiwanese, and Filipino parents and grandparents of my friends will retain a righteous hatred of the Japanese for the colonial sins and war crimes inflicted upon their countries. I know it makes little sense, but I feel responsible for any acts my military ancestors may have committed in the name of nationalism and duty, and I am still too afraid to learn the truth of what they did or did not do to go digging up family histories. We indeed are all "by-products of the mid-twentieth century," as Ozeki writes, and I irrationally and grandiosely fear that like microplastics, like neo-imperial structures of power, like the internet, I too am circulating some insidious unknown poison as I move through the world.

I wonder what my dad knew or believed about his family and refused to tell us, and why, but now he is too sunk in Alzheimer's to give us real answers even if he wanted to. I grew up accustomed to the unreality of our family in Japan, so their historical absence was normal to me. But I do wish I could see, again, that photo my grandmother kept or even summon up the boy's face. I've forgotten exactly what he looked like. Instead, I fill in the faces from the glossy photo inserts of history books or Google Image searches for terms like "Japanese WWII pilot" or "tokkōtai pilot" or "kamikaze pilot." All these portraits fit the frame of the photo I've forgotten: a boy pilot in a bright scarf, very alive, very young.

I have no way of knowing what kind of pilot my grandmother's brother actually was, or whether his plane crashed by mandated suicide. I cannot know if he believed in the imperialist regime he died for, or who he was otherwise. But when I read Ozeki he blurred into a character from *A Tale for the Time Being*. In the book, one of its two narrators, Naoko Yasutani, discovers that her great-uncle Haruki was a pilot in the tokkōtai program—the "Special Attack Force," more infamously known outside Japan as the kamikaze, or "divine wind." He was also a pacifist comparative literature student drafted into military service against his will and his conscience. Like my great-uncle, Haruki died in a plane, but by water, not fire, crashing into the waves of the Pacific when he refuses to aim at his target and kill innocent people. His ghost comes back to meet Nao kindly at Obon, the Japanese holiday when the dead go on summer vacation and come back to visit the living. I grabbed on to Haruki's ghost desperately, wanting to believe that some part of my dad's family might be recuperable, too; that some of our history could be redeemed.

So, from the beginning, this novel was a *lot*.

This was not the only aspect of the book that reached into me, deeply and immediately. The book's two protagonists also might seem like they are engineered to appeal to a reader of my particular specifications. The first, Nao, is a depressed (but charming!) Japanese teenager unwillingly repatriated to Tokyo after growing up in California in the South Bay—in the same town where my then-boyfriend grew up. The second, Ruth, is a middle-aged writer, a Japanese American Canadian like me, and a longtime New Yorker now living on a tiny island off the coast of British Columbia. This Ruth is and is not Ruth Ozeki, with whom she shares much in common, including the name of her husband, Oliver, her vocation as a novelist, and the fact of her mother's death from Alzheimer's. Suicide is present from page one: Nao, who we meet first, addresses the reader who she imagines will find the diary she's writing, referring to it as "the diary of my last days on earth." She's not sure if the reader will stay with her until the end.

Nao's dad is also depressed and tries to kill himself several times in the book. The facts of this father-daughter relationship are drastically different from mine with my father; Nao and her dad were close when they lived in California but grow distant when they return to Japan, whereas my dad and I only ever shared the aggressive, unidirectional intimacy of parental expectation and pressure. Nao's sadness is her own, but it's also her father's. I have felt sometimes like my sadness might have been my father's sadness, but more often I felt that my sadness was born out of his rage, like a genetic flaw that got somehow twisted in replication. I did feel a twinge of recognition in Nao's despair as she looks at her dad, not understanding why he is the way he is. And all of us, all four of us, in different ways, carried the weight of being Japanese and some kind of American, not knowing what either of those things should mean to us in either place—how much shame? How much love?

"There is too much self in my writing," Anne Carson says in her study of Paul Celan, *Economy of the Unlost*. With Ozeki's book, like many of the others I've invoked here, there is too much self in my reading.

*

The novel is too full of stuff, like the ocean. Too many things wash up on the shores of Desolation Sound, where Ruth lives in a tiny, remote community: "The sea was always heaving things up and hurling them back: fishing lines, floats, beer cans, plastic toys, tampons, Nike sneakers. A few years earlier it was severed feet." Too many things that speak of human violence and waste, whether the sneaker or the foot; too many signs of the human infiltration of the sea, the most unknowable part of the once-natural world. The plot of the novel hinges upon this oversaturation, via a very contemporary version of the traditional message in a bottle. One day, Ruth discovers a mysterious trove of materials washed up on the beach, packaged in a red Hello Kitty lunch box, kept safe in layers and layers of plastic. Inside, she finds Nao's handwritten diary, along with Haruki's letters home from training and his army-issued watch. This discovery establishes a deceptively simple format for this complicated novel. It's structured as a back-and-forth between sections of Nao's diary, written circa 2003, and a third-person narrative of Ruth's experience reading and researching the diary and its writer in 2012. But the mysterious circumstances of the lunch box's arrival cannot be forgotten, and immediately broaden the scope of the story, to include not only Nao and Ruth, but the ocean itself and its ever-turning gyres. The novel takes all of this and sweeps it into its own gyre, dense with the particulate matter of ideas, history, time, being, love, death. It should be totally overwhelming and it is—but also somehow, reading it, it's not.

Here is a very partial list of things that Ozeki manages to meaningfully discuss (or at least make the reader curious about) in *A Tale for the Time Being:*

The Great Pacific Garbage Patch, species of crows and ravens, instructions for *zazen*, a history of the Japanese I-novel, 9/11, Schrödinger's cat, Alzheimer's disease, an explanation of how many moments there are in a day (6,400,099,980), marriage, cats, the NeoEocene, a partial geography of British Columbia's Sunshine Coast, otaku culture, life on a tiny island, Japanese ideas about suicide, how depressing writing is, Edith Piaf, how ocean currents work, a 104-year-old Buddhist nun, bullying (*ijime*, 虐め) in Japanese schools, quantum physics, the biography of physicist Hugh Everett, translation, the internet, the tech boom, Y2K, ghosts of the living and the dead, the Sendai earthquake and Fukushima meltdown, the Zen concept of nonbeing (*mu*, 無), kamikaze pilots, *Sein und Zeit*, anarchist feminist Kanno Sugako, *hikikomori*, Marcel Proust.

It was all there, and it was all so clear! It was all too much, and yet somehow the novel made it seem like there was ample space for all these intense things—and so much more—to stretch out. I too had a feeling of profound too-muchness, but I never had enough mental space to sort it all out. My mind felt full, too full, of ideas and stories—mine, my family's and friends', from books. Sometimes this felt exhilarating, sometimes frightening, sometimes just like a headache. I wondered if I had a brain tumor, or inanely, if my thoughts could *become* a brain tumor. I always thought that if, like an air mattress, I could somehow find a big release valve (one of my ears maybe) and let all the things filling my head out with a *whoosh*, I would feel less bloated, my head empty in a healthy way, ready to be filled again with new thoughts, new stories.

When it was very bad, I felt it in my skin. After I started my teaching job in 2013, as I worked endlessly on my ill-fated academic book, I began to feel like I was bloating, swelling grossly like a sausage in a hot pan, my thoughts proliferating too fast for my body to contain them. There were too many ideas to write out, and I never had enough interior space for each of them to fully unfold. They just collected and built up, so that my entire body felt full of them, tight and painful. I would occasionally feel a slight relief when I finished an article or presented a paper at a conference; I could almost see the mental edema go down in my hands or face. But overnight the ideas would collect and the feeling of horrible tautness would build again. I couldn't look at my face in these moments; it was unrecognizably swollen, stretched to its limit and about to tear. In response to these fantasies, my eczema, which had disfigured my fingers when I was a small child to the point that I had to wear vaselined vinyl gloves to school, returned with vigor, so that my hands looked the way I imagined my whole body might, the skin filled with tiny bubbles of fluid that would burst and crack.

Ozeki's novel took that ugly, grotesque feeling and made it beautiful. Because at its heart, under the complicating, intellectually heady elements of its dabbling in quantum mechanics and Zen thought, *A Tale for the Time Being* is really the story of too-muchness metamorphosing into transcendent connection: of a family mending many threads of connection that they did not even realize were broken. Not only do Nao and Jiko, her Buddhist nun great-grandmother, find out the truth of what happened to Haruki, that truth also reunites Nao and her father, who have been drifting further and further apart on the currents of their own despair, and saves them both. The book ultimately performs a healing, exorcising recuperation of the family that makes me long for one of my own and believe that it could happen somehow, someday. It was my own dream come to life; a book—Nao's diary—does in fact save her and her whole family, both the living and the dead.

This all comes to pass through the mystical intervention of Ruth, the reader of Nao's story, who magically participates in the piecing together of the Yasutani family's shared tale of mourning and melancholia from afar. The diary saves her and Oliver as well. It helps her finally begin to process her mother's last years and her loss; as she gets more and more involved, the processes of reading and producing the text become inextricably intertwined. It kicked up my faith in a book that could save me. That faith had been flagging, but it was not quite dead. And indeed, when I first started reading the novel and writing about it, which I did several times between 2013 and 2017 in different academic contexts, I had an exhilaratingly paranoid sensation that matched up with Ruth's feeling in the book—that Nao's diary was somehow listening, responding to her own reading of it. The novel expands and expands, its knotted-up threads proliferating on their own, twisting together and tendriling off as they grow. It was so much, so greedy for more information and more coincidence, so vibrant and shockingly alive that I felt that way, too.

Somehow, against the rules of genre and physics, this novel was capacious enough to hold the too-much. My brain was not, but Ozeki gave me hope that it could be. Her book made salvation seem possible. "You're my kind of time being and together we'll make magic!" Nao promises the reader at the beginning. Perhaps, I thought for the first time in a long time, I could even save myself by reading it, by writing about it, by mere proximity to this magic.

There's a part at the beginning of *How Should a Person Be?* where Sheila Heti muses about her most frequent typo: When she means to type "soul" she types "sould." It's loaded in all the ways you can imagine. I do this too, almost every time. Another Freudian typo that I make almost daily: "world" for "word" and vice versa. Ozeki, like so many seductively great novelists, made them seem like they could be the same thing.

*

I'm losing track of what I'm supposed to be doing here. What I have to tell you is not too much—in fact, it's barely anything at all. I just need to explain how I got from reading Carson in Oxford in August 2018 to the inpatient psychiatry unit at Tisch Hospital in February 2019. This is not a good story, and I must constantly resist the urge to make it one. That's the annoying fact that challenges all writing about depression: It is just not a good story. It usually does not have a clearly defined beginning or ending; it's mostly just terrible, boring middle after terrible, boring middle. One assumes that a lot of dramatic stuff must have been going on, but as far as I can remember, nothing really happened between summer and winter. I did have a contained meltdown on the bus from Oxford to Heathrow—imagine a fit of poorly contained, seat-racking sobs that deeply embarrassed the coachload of English people who were stuck with me for an uncomfortable hour and a half—but as soon as I landed at JFK, I went back to business as scheduled. I mechanically advised freshmen on their schedules, fretted over my academic book, wrote letters of recommendation. I told myself everything was fine, until suddenly it wasn't.

When I look back at it, it seems oddly like the biggest change that occurred over those months was a change in interpretation: that sometimes joyful feeling of the too-much made miraculously manageable by *A Tale for the Time Being* (and, in its way, by "The Glass Essay") simply felt like *too much* again and managing it seemed like it had been a stupid fantasy in the first place. The too-much overwhelmed me so wholly that it started to look like its other side—nothing.

I looked back at my emails from the weeks of my breakdown, but you can barely tell that anything happened. Things went wrong the night of February 2; there's a break of about a day and a half there. But then, the day I allowed myself to be taken to the hospital, February 4, there are a bunch of work emails sent during the night that I spent under observation, in a brightly lit cage-like room in the ER. What would happen to my classes? Could I get short-term disability for this? Would one freshman advisee get into her second-choice writing seminar, and would another be able to get on the waiting list for the course that I suddenly, probably, wouldn't be teaching? They took my phone and computer away for the first couple of days when I was admitted; another short break. But then it's a nonstop flurry of work emails, most of them obsequiously apologetic. I remember working at my desk in the shared hospital room (why do they even have desks in there if they don't want you to keep working?). I was desperate to get out as fast as possible and probably left far too early, after only a week, because I was so worried about work. The morning I got out, as I was waiting for Merve to come pick me up from the billing office, I wrote cravenly to a colleague who wanted to meet: "So sorry, I'm going through a weird medical thing (nothing to worry about) and am going to try and take a few days completely off!" One might think that I'd broken my leg, not my brain. Knowing what a gap there was between what was really happening and how I made it seem makes it a vertiginous read.

With horrible felicity, I was supposed to be writing about *A Tale for the Time Being*, revising a series of conference papers into one long peer-reviewed article that would eventually—hopefully sooner rather than later—make itself useful as a chapter in my monograph. But no matter how hard I tried, I could not make myself go back through my papers and confront my stupid, optimistic ideas about the novel. I could not read the novel page by page, any more than I could read any novel then. The best I could do was scroll aimlessly through the six-page single-spaced Word doc that contained all the quotes from the book that I really wanted to address.

The novel doesn't ever want to stop—part of its too-muchness—and following its fairly conventional, mostly happy ending, it has a fully peacemaking epilogue, six appendices, and a bibliography. The sixth of these short appendices is a condensed, tragic biography of Hugh Everett, the quantum physicist who published the "many worlds" theory (it was his doctoral thesis at, of all places, Princeton). He was laughed out of academia and went to work for the Pentagon's Weapons Systems Evaluation Group, where he was responsible for writing code to target population centers with atomic weapons during the Cold War. Ozeki's crushing portrait in miniature makes him sound like a bitter nihilist who destroyed himself and his family: "He'd already written the mathematical proof of his many-worlds interpretation, and he believed that anything he could imagine would occur, or already had. It's not surprising that he drank heavily." His daughter, Liz, attempted suicide early on and after her father's death (after which his wife kept his ashes in a filing cabinet for a while and then put them in the garbage, as he'd wished) she tried again and succeeded. The appendix reproduces her suicide note in full, and it offers the very last words of the novel:

> Please burn me and DON'T FILE ME ☺. Please sprinkle me in some nice body of water ... or the garbage, maybe that way I'll end up in the correct parallel universe to meet up w/Daddy.

Rereading these words, I suddenly felt so stupid. How could I have ever thought that the novel gave hope, when its last lines are so full of despair, despair made even more despairing by its faux cheeriness? I thought about my own frenetically upbeat hospital emails for a while, and then about why Ozeki put Liz's note where she put it. The book potentially ends so many times; the reader is given a choice about which of these moments is the last one to them, the last one they think counts. I thought of Everett's possible worlds. In one of them, *A Tale for the Time Being* ends happily. In another, it ends in this total despair. For years I had chosen to believe that the happy ending to the plot was the real ending, with Ruth having saved Nao through textual-astral-Zen-quantum-mechanical means ("together we'll make magic!"). I believed this willfully because it made the too-muchness bearable, even tellable and resolvable. It was a magical reading and it made me feel like some kind of magical intervention might make life equally resolvable.

But when I considered the whole thing again, the impossibility of it all—of narrative recuperation—seemed so foolish and naïve. I thought of the famous line at the end of Ian McEwan's *Atonement,* another book where an author's desire to resolve life through fiction-making fails. "The attempt was all," she says, hoping for forgiveness. I didn't buy it in *Atonement* (where the whole point was not to buy it) and I ceased to buy it in Ozeki. The attempt was unethical. The attempt was impossible. The attempt was stupid, and in the end, the attempt to just write it all out and fix it in prose was the same as giving up and erasing it all.

There was no controlling the too-muchness of real life. It would invariably overflow and drown you from the inside out; Ruth and Nao could only survive it and make it work for them because they were characters, novelistic contrivances that, despite how much Ruth looked like Ozeki, would never have to live our terrible, overspilling lives. The word was not the world and it never had been.

*

This summer I really reread Ozeki for the first time in years as Obon approached: The feeling of too-muchness was everywhere. As Nao writes in her diary, "the hot air felt pregnant with ghosts." I could feel them stirring faintly in the humid slog—did they wish they could be reborn into this overfull world? Or were they happier as they were, moving on the currents of the air and sea?

Wondering about them, I thought back to a brilliant and moving meditation on the life and work of the leftist feminist thinker Barbara Ehrenreich that I'd read several months ago, by the labor historian Gabriel Winant. At the very end, he turns to a piece of Ehrenreich's writing I'd never seen before, her 1987 foreword to Klaus Theweleit's *Male Fantasies*. She exhorts us to pay attention to ourselves, and to how we read, and in so doing, be receptive and give in to the moments where

the dams break. Curiosity swims upstream and turns around, surprising itself. Desire streams forth through the channels of imagination. Barriers—between women and men, the "high" and the "low"—crumble in the face of this new energy. This is what the fascist held himself in horror of, and what he saw in communism, in female sexuality—a joyous commingling, as disorderly as life. In this fantasy, the body expands, in its senses, its imaginative reach—to fill the earth. And we are at last able to rejoice in the softness and the permeability of the world around us, rather than holding ourselves back in lonely dread. This is the fantasy that makes us, both men and women, human—and makes us, sometimes, revolutionaries in the cause of life.

I thought about my old feeling of too-muchness, and what it would mean to surrender to that "softness and permeability" that Ehrenreich describes. To be permeable to the tides of story and history, to let everything that feels like too much flow freely through the mind and body. This is the way to live joyfully and defiantly, whether in politics or in the individual mind. This is the only way to escape the rule of the pre-ordained, damning plotlines that expand to fit whatever empty hollows they are allowed and can exert so much painful pressure when we try to control or undo them.

Here is a partial list of things that came into this chapter and had to be removed again because they were too much, and I'm trying to let that be okay; things that I had to live with for a while and let go of because I really, truly am trying to accept that sometimes you just *must*, trusting that someday they will all come back to you again:

Nagarjuna, the Great Pacific Garbage Patch, Elena Ferrante's concept of *frantumaglia*, nurdles, A. S. Byatt's "Sea Story," Donovan Hohn's *Moby-Duck*, Emiko Ohnuki-Tierney's *Kamikaze, Cherry Blossoms, and Nationalisms* and *Kamikaze Diaries*, why I believe in ghosts, the apocalypse, Frank Kermode's *The Sense of an Ending*, "hysterical realism," Bernie Sanders, the internet, "too much crying" according to Merve, W. B. Yeats, the Sendai earthquake and Fukushima meltdown, Rob Nixon's *Slow Violence*, Ruth's mom's Alzheimer's, my dad's Alzheimer's, a cruel relationship and terrible breakup, more family feuds, the Heart Sutra, Lou Harrison's setting for choir and American Gamelan of the Heart Sutra (translated, touchingly, into Esperanto as *Lo Koro Sutro*), *Sein-zum-Tode*, Dōgen Zenji, Sarah Manguso's *The Guardians*, my red Mole-

skine planner from 2019, Toni Morrison's *Jazz*, my mom, 9/11,
Marcel Proust.

The too-much is part of life, I tell myself now. The too-
much *is* life, and so is the nothing. (I have to keep telling
myself this.)

*

But I can't make this revelation matter to what happened
then. I can sit and rethink how the novel works and ruefully
critique the story I was writing about myself, reread my emails
and try to remember in every detail what I was doing, who I
was writing to, why I was so afraid of dropping any balls. But
I can't do anything about it, and I can't make anything make
sense, nor should it; I also can't go back in time and tell myself
that it was futile to try and make sense of it at all. It's like
skipping around in a home movie; little details get caught out
of order and the whole thing is too long and too shameful to
sit through because you can't ever change it. I can never find
the moment I'm looking for. I keep accidentally holding down
fast-forward and skipping to the end, so I watch that over and
over again, not sure if I can get anything out of it, not sure
why I'm doing it. It's become a compulsion, thinking through
that night before the hospital.

It was the coldest day of the year.* I had just sent off the
revision of an academic essay, after tearing my hair out over

---

* I remember it being the coldest day of the year, though when I look it up,
the coldest day of 2019 in New York was apparently January 31. But on February 2, it was still historically cold as the polar vortex settled in over the city, so
I might as well let drama win.

the editing process. Bibliophobia had set in in August when I came back from Oxford and Carson and had been worsening for months, so I'd dully answered the editor's queries, unable to write whole new sentences. It hadn't been a great day, but it hadn't been the worst; I'd gotten work done, and I had dinner plans with friends. I put on a lot of ugly layers and my hideous sleeping bag coat (for emergency use only) to tackle the mile walk to Matt and Rachel's apartment to eat pasta with them and our friend Adam. We had a good night, a night so warm and fun that I placidly let Adam convince me to meet up with some people at a show. When I protested that I wasn't ready to see anyone, Rachel dressed me up like a doll in her clothes. The show was great. We met our friends and walked to Jared and Monica's nearby apartment after and drank whiskey and watched stupid videos on YouTube until 3:00 A.M., the traditional last moment to leave somewhere on a Saturday night and head home sanely, without ruining Sunday.

A few of us walked out of the building together. The cold bit through our coats, and as they got in a waiting Lyft, they asked if I would call a car. I told them I wanted to walk a bit and promised it would only be to the next subway, no farther. We embraced and parted ways.

I felt good and extra-lucid and bright as I started off up Broadway. I peered up at the sky, framed on one side by the elevated tracks, as a few of those pinprick-tiny snowflakes began to fall—the random ones you get when it's too cold to really snow—glittering in the golden light of the streetlamp. The one thing I remembered from high school chemistry was that sodium-vapor lights gave off amber light, while mercury-vapor lights were cool and blue-toned, and I always thought of them as sunlight and moonlight. How lucky, I thought,

snow falling through the sun in the dead of night. The warmth
I had felt from being with my friends continued to burn inside me. I passed the Myrtle Avenue JMZ subway stop, then
Flushing Avenue. I'm practically halfway there, I thought
with deliberate inaccuracy, I might as well go on.

But before I got to the Lorimer stop, I started to feel tears
rolling down my cold cheeks. I couldn't understand why I was
crying, and that made me cry harder. The onslaught was astonishing: so immediate, so unexpected I couldn't even re-
direct my energy into trying to make it stop. Automatically, I
just kept trudging along. Suddenly, somehow, I was weeping
so hard it clearly terrified the very occasional walkers I passed
along the way. A drunk-seeming guy put his arm around his
also drunk-seeming girlfriend, and they unsteadily picked
their way across the empty street as I trudged toward them,
not even trying to quiet my sobs. I keened into the night air
and didn't care if people heard, which felt amazing. I remember that moment as if I could see myself from outside so
clearly—it was the precise moment that I realized that I did
not care who saw because I had lost my mind. I screamed
once experimentally. And again, longer. Nobody would even
notice; it was New York.

What had happened? Nothing. I think that was the problem. If I could have a wonderful night with my friends and
still be overwhelmed by nothing at all, still feel like nothing
was simply too much—well, it was all over.

So, it was all over.

I decided as suddenly and as unthinkingly as I did when I
was ten, gulping down that handful of Tylenol gelcaps. The
decision had been so close ever since then—always just an
extra-long breath away. I felt a deep, familiar relief that it was

finally here, after more than twenty-five years. I stopped at the overpass at Marcy and looked down at the cars and trucks traversing the BQE. By that time, it must have been 4:00 A.M.; I was surprised to see that there was still a diminished but streaming flow of traffic. I climbed up on the low, square rail that sat inside the slightly arched chain-link fence lining the overpass. The knit of the fence was a little tight; the holes were snug but my gloved fingers fit in them perfectly. I stood like that for a while, looking down at the trucks as they carried things in and out of the city. This was not the way, obviously. The fence was a little too high, and it wasn't very far down, only maybe twenty or twenty-five feet, and anyway, to jump into traffic was just about the worst thing to do—it would cause an accident, and even if there were no other injuries at this hour, it would ruin some poor sap's life. I stood there a while longer, though, because it felt good and free.

I climbed down and sat on the sidewalk for a minute or ten. I was suddenly tired, but my body wanted to walk, so I got up and let it. It wanted to go down to the water, which suddenly felt like the obvious place to go. Books came streaming into my mind as I contemplated what cross street would take me to the riverside, both idly and horribly distracting. The East River, I'd recently learned, was a saltwater estuary, not a river. Practically the ocean, I thought. How correct that was. I thought of Liz Everett's note: "Please sprinkle me in some nice body of water." The East River is also a drowned valley; I thought of the drowned Welsh village in W. G. Sebald's *Austerlitz*, the Lost Land in Susan Cooper's *Silver on the Tree*, the glass-cheeked ladies in Byatt's underwater City of Is. The texts kept crowding in eagerly, as if they knew this was their last chance. I thought of the winter carnival in Vir-

ginia Woolf's *Orlando,* when the Thames freezes so deep and
clear that an apple seller on the deck of a sunken ship can be
seen through the icy fathoms, looking alive and well but for "a
certain blueness about the lips." I hoped fancifully that I
would be the same and then thought of Laura Palmer's awful,
fascinating beauty when her corpse washes up in the first episode of *Twin Peaks.*

I thought of Woolf, with a regrettable sigh; surely, I would
now be tarred as a sad Woolf fangirl to my academic peers, an
unsuccessful modernist. A faint bitterness arose, and I tried to
let it go, to let it drift away before the end. I thought of the
ghost of Hamlet's father, who died "unhousel'd, disappointed,
unaneled." I wanted to die shriven of my scholarly failings. I
had to stop thinking of Hamlet or the allusions would never
stop. The books had to stop; this all had to stop. The too-
muchness was coming on and I felt a rising wildness.

I thought of Virginia's note to Leonard: "I am doing what
seems the best thing to do."

But then the thought of a note made me think of my cat. I
pictured him as he must have been at that moment, curled on
the bed without me. He was always so hungry, or said he was.
Every cat has a catchphrase; Swinton's was "How *dare* you!" I
had fed him before I went out that night, but he would still be
up in a flash to crossly convince me otherwise if I were to go
home and turn on the lights, even if it were 4:30 and he'd just
emerged from wherever cats go in their deepest sleeps. If I
didn't go back and then wasn't found for a couple of days,
would somebody think to go and check on him? And someone would have to take care of him after, too; he had a ton of
allergies and the complicated formula of raw food, grain-free
dry food, ample fresh water, and poultry-free treats that kept

him happy and digestively competent had been painstakingly titrated over the course of many years but never committed to paper. For the sake of his continued health and the benefit of amateur feline dietitians everywhere, I had to write a note. It is undeniably ludicrous that my suicide note was just going to be a meticulous cat-care manual, but also so purely practical it scares me; it's so terribly matter-of-fact. It did not seem silly to me at all at the time.*

The thought of it all was exhausting. The cold had, by this time, made my head feel numb, and that numbness was something like sleepiness. I had not slept for several days and there was, I calculated, still at least a half-hour walk back to the very top of Greenpoint. I realized that I didn't ever want to go back there, to the dark, narrow hallway of a rent-stabilized railroad apartment where over the course of the last several years, I'd slid down some unseen embankment to the narrow edge where I found myself teetering now. I'd loved that apartment so much when I first moved in—the first place that really felt like it was mine—and I thought I would live there forever, like the old Polish lady on the top floor who died in the hallway the month after I arrived. The best feature was a tall 1920s built-in cabinet, which I filled with double- and triple-deep rows of books. But the place had grown darker and more haunted in recent months espe-

---

* It briefly occurred to me in this moment that at the beginning of *A Tale for the Time Being*, Nao asks, "Do you have a cat and is she sitting on your lap? Does her forehead smell like cedar trees and fresh sweet air?" Yes, says Ruth at the end, "How did you know?" Yes exactly, I thought, how did you know? But Swinton's delicately tweeded orange forehead always smelled of cinnamon and soft new bread. I was not Ruth; the book was not speaking to me, and never had been.

cially; it grew hoardery-dense with too many books to shelve, with too many frightening feelings and memories. I'd just have to go back this once and write my cat manual, and while I was at it, I thought, clear up some other business; burn the letter to an ex that I'd drafted but never sent, double-check that I'd assigned Becca as the beneficiary on my retirement and life insurance policies, leave instructions on the apartment door. At least the rent was paid already; it was the beginning of the month, and it would surely take some time to clean out the place. I'd go home and do these necessary tasks and, since the winter ferry schedule would not accommodate my plans—it *was* sad, I thought rather peevishly, not to get a last ferry ride—I'd get on the G to the A and take it all the way out to the Rockaways before the sun rose. Because really, who needed the shitty old East River that wasn't even a river when the all-consuming ocean was right there.

It was too cold to take out my phone and check the time. It was still far from dawn, I thought. I had hours yet to make my way back there if I needed them. I wished I had a cigarette for this; I'd always loved smoking in winter, when the smell of smoke was rendered somehow bitter-clean by the frigid air. I was so tired, and this last mile was so far. I trudged up South Third toward Berry, taking tiny stiff steps like an arthritic toy dog; my long down coat, zipped all the way to the calf, felt like it was suddenly constricting my stride. I had plenty of time, I thought, I can just take a rest here. A low, red-brown stone stoop presented itself to me, its two broad, shallow steps looking wonderfully clean and smooth. I have all the time in the world, I thought, suddenly sanguine, bending down to sit. It felt so good that I lay down on my side. As I sank into the deep down of my coat, my large hood folded over my face,

shutting out the street; I could only see a slice of the pavement, lit golden and serene. I'll just close my eyes for a minute, I thought, my warm breath filling the fleecy inside of my
hood-cave. I felt my muscles unwind just a little, and in that
moment the relief was the greatest thing I'd ever felt. I thought
fleetingly of my favorite movie title as I closed my eyes, Pow-
ell and Pressburger's *I Know Where I'm Going!* For once I too
knew where I was going and just then—just then—everything
was exactly enough.

Chapter 7

UNQUIET GRAVES

One of my most treasured childhood books was my mom's copy of *The Joan Baez Songbook,* a brittle, yellowed folio that had traveled in her guitar case through the folk scene of Toronto in the late sixties. When I was very small, I confused Joan Baez with my mother; they both had long black hair and sad, kind eyes. In Baez's book were a number of the Child Ballads, from the volumes of English and Scottish folk songs collected by Francis James Child, Harvard's first professor of English, in the late nineteenth century. I read these lyrics over and over again, obsessed with their repeating cycles of love and death, love and death. My favorite ones were the supernatural ballads, stories of demon lovers and ghosts and the Devil himself, on sabbatical from Hell. My very favorite was "The Unquiet Grave," Child number 78. It is, for lack of a better term, *a mood:*

> Cold blows the wind to my true love
> And gently drops the rain

I've never had but one true love
And in green-wood he lies slain

I'll do as much for my true love
As any young girl may
I'll sit and mourn all on his grave
For twelve months and a day.

And when twelve months and a day was passed,
The ghost did rise and speak:
"Why sittest thou all on my grave,
And will not let me sleep?"

There are two lovers, one left alive at the headstone, the other dead in the grave. The living awaits the dead, grieving for a year and a day without cease. The ghost then returns to ask why his mourner will not leave. A series of riddles follows, their phrases opaque and totemic:

Go fetch me water from the desert
And blood from out the stone
Go fetch me milk from a fair maid's breast
That a young man never has known.

The impossible images are strange and their purpose unclear. The ballad is fragmented and the dialogue between the living and dead is jumbled, leaving the meaning uncertain; the only thing that is clear is that they will never again be together in this world. I loved the song's atmosphere of unearthly melancholy, of hopeless desolation. I repeated certain phrases: Blood from a stone. Twelve months and a day. Cold blows the wind. "The Unquiet Grave" stayed with me, perhaps the first poem to do so. I'm not sure why, but it was a poem I didn't share with anyone—it felt necessarily lonely, as if it were only written there for me, even though I understood, at a distance, that it was a folk song that had reached me through many thousands of unknown voices and hands, including my mother's.

Years later, in college, one of my jobs was in an underground library, a fluorescent-lit tomb for books and wan nocturnal paper writers. The easiest but dullest shift on the schedule was "shelf reading": sitting in one section and scanning the call numbers to make sure that the books were in perfect Library of Congress order. Late one night, skimming along somewhere in the PRs, I came across the large, occultish, black-bound volumes of the Child Ballads. I turned to number 78 and found that Baez's telling was missing verses, in which the mourner answers the ghost's question, beseechingly,

> "'Tis I, my love, sits on your grave,
> And will not let you sleep;
> For I crave one kiss of your clay-cold lips;
> And that is all I seek."

To which the ghost replies with a warning,

> "You crave one kiss of my clay-cold lips;
> But my breath smells earthy strong;
> If you have one kiss of my clay-cold lips,
> Your time will not be long."

I sat alone in an empty aisle as I mouthed these words. I could feel the silent regard of the other books that surrounded me as I bent over the Child Ballads' thick, foxed pages, their loamy scent richer than the dry vented air of the library. Holding the book in my hands I felt, horribly and deliciously, like I held the hand of the ghostly lover. I looked up to catch my breath and was startled by my own huddled reflection in the darkness of the floor-to-ceiling window at the end of the aisle—exactly the kind of horror movie window where pale faces are inclined to appear. I shivered and reshelved the volume, then skittered back to the circulation desk, leaving the rest of my shelf irresponsibly unread. (Unsurprisingly, I was fired a few weeks later, when, during another failed shelf-reading shift, I was apprehended while stuffed cravenly into one of the tiny study closets everyone called "weenie bins," reading an Anne Rice novel.)

Still more years later, I opened a book of essays by an author I'd heard of but never read before and met "The Unquiet Grave" again. I felt the tingle of static shock as I turned to the first page and read,

> "The wind doth blow today, my love,
> And a few small drops of rain;
> I never had but one true-love,
> In cold grave she was lain.
>
> "I'll do as much for my true-love
> As any young man may;
> I'll sit and mourn all at her grave
> For a twelvemonth and a day."

Then a narrator picks up the story:

> The twelvemonth and a day being up, I was still at a
> loss. If anything I was more at a loss.
>   So I went and stood in our study and looked at your
> desk, where the unfinished stuff, what you'd been work-
> ing on last, was still neatly piled. I looked at your books,
> I took one of your books off a shelf at random—*my*
> study, *my* desk, *my* books, now.

The unnamed narrator begins to read the book—*Oliver
Twist*—but is interrupted shortly by a ghostly visitor:

> . . . I looked up over the top of the open book because
> it sounded like someone was coming up the stairs.
>   Someone was. It was you.

Reading this rewriting of familiar words then, I was in-
trigued and excitingly unsettled, as I always am upon discovering that someone shares one of my minute personal
obsessions. Rereading it now, sitting alone amid my own
books, I am extra-attuned to the vibrations of the uncanny, as
the book's and the ballad's scenes of waiting, mourning, reading pile up on my own, like the sheaf of pages on the abandoned desk. That first time and this time, and every reading in
between, despite the fact that I know what I will find when I
turn that first page, I feel a little shiver as I read those familiar
words and think for a moment that I see a face at the window,
a figure in the doorway. I am drawn into the limbo of the
scene: between life and death, familiar words and unfamiliar
ones, between writing and reading.

The book is *Artful,* by the Scottish novelist and critic Ali Smith. *Artful* itself began life as a series of lectures that Smith gave as a visiting professor of comparative literature at Oxford. I love imagining the scene of the acclaimed writer walking up to the lectern in front of a very serious crowd of students and faculty to deliver some solemn remarks on literature, then unexpectedly launching into a ghost story, like a character in a staid period drama suddenly breaking into a TikTok dance.

It's impossible to define *Artful* in generic terms. It's a ghost story, a love story, a slippery series of associative readings, a mourning diary, a loosely knit work of criticism sequined with slivers of fiction, fragments of theory. When I taught it in seminar, my students couldn't figure out what to call it—they often slipped up and called it a novel and would correct themselves to say essays, lectures, or just "pieces." Ultimately, we started calling it, first as a joke, then seriously, an "item of mortality." This is a phrase Dickens uses to describe the infant Oliver, but in addition to a baby, Smith reminds us, it could also mean more—as she writes, "the item of mortality could mean the whole book, like I was somehow holding an item of mortality in my hands."

This item of mortality spoke with a voice that kept shifting, from the unnamed storyteller, to the ghost of the critic, perhaps to Ali Smith herself or someone like her, and in each form, it drew me in closer. It was the spectral lover I'd been waiting for, waiting for for far longer than a twelvemonth and a day—or maybe I was the ghost, summoned by this strange, lively book. This book seemed to know me, and know what I wanted, better than I did myself. My jealous and desirous feelings roiled more violently, and then got mixed in with a new, odder feeling that there was no point writing anymore, because Ali Smith had already written the book I'd been longing to write. I got confused. I felt lost in it, a feeling that I can only think of through an image from *Artful* itself:

> In my sleep, I would stand up from the desk and pull on a coat. . . . I'd open the coat and run my hand down its inside lining, full of hidden pockets and compartments. I'd put my hand into one and pull out—what? a hand, on the end of an arm—a limb. A passport into limbo. The hand at the end of the arm would speak through a mouth made of thumb and first finger. You need to take me with you, it would say, so you don't come to no arm.
>
>   I'd pick it up and slip it back into its pocket and the hand, holding my own hand, would pull me deeper . . .

The passage pulls me in in just the way it describes, and I feel like I could fall deeper and deeper into the mysterious pocket-limbo of the book and never emerge. I am enamored by these words and long to do as they command; reading it and typing it feels like grasping the hand and letting it pull me, willing and unwitting, wherever it wants to go. It disarms me.

Ha. I am playing the text's game—but am I playing it right? Will I ever be able to pull back on that guiding hand with equal strength and certainty, or will it always be the one leading me? Reading *Artful,* I began to understand the anxiety that had been building around my reading practice for a long time: the fear that my confusion of the text with the reader is an unhealthy mingling of life and death. I get lost in this feeling and start to wonder if I am a real, living person.

So much of the reading I do is kneeling at the graveside, waiting for something to reemerge and take me down with it—to *ghost* me, not in the casual abandonment sense of the term, but by taking me away from life and sweeping me into the dark void of whatever lies beyond the page. "The Unquiet Grave" staged a scene that I found myself reenacting time and time again, waiting for the text in my hands to come to life and draw me in. I am very afraid that casting myself into this willing suspension between life and death betrays nothing more than some sick fascination with dead things. I wonder yet again if it is possible to unpick the knots that tie my reading habits to my depression. At times, especially when I was younger, reading felt to me pleasantly like dangling one foot in the grave; I would read all day and all night the way some other depressives I've known might sleep whole weeks away. In the most unbearable periods, it was a way to not live in my life, to not live in my body, to not live at all, but also not be entirely outside of it, not yet anyway. I don't think this was simply escapism; I don't remember ever feeling like I was really living in the alternate universe of the book. It felt—still often feels—so good to just be a ghost that haunts the world of the text, visible neither here nor there. To linger in the meeting of the living and the dead, in the very moment when warm, live lips touch clay-cold, dead ones, a moment without a future. I read to be on the cusp.

And now, inhabiting words that I wish I had written—or, in sublime, alarming moments of entranced reading, that I *experience writing*—is what makes me a spectral presence, not

a living body. This is yet another manifestation of my bibliophobia, and like all the others it is so obviously laced with
desire. As my craving for this feeling increases, so does my
fear of becoming a ghost of someone else's book forever, with
no words—and thus no life!—of my own.

*

What it feels like is in between: in between reading and writing, in between my mind and the author's, in between life and
death. It feels safe to be in between, where no one else can
find you. That's where I found myself as the sun rose—with
what seemed like unnatural slowness—after that cold night. I
had fallen asleep for a while (a minute? an hour or two?) on
that stoop, and when I awoke, I couldn't feel my skin. That
sensation, or weird lack of sensation, was all I recall. I don't
remember how I got that last mile home; I imagine myself
lurching up Franklin Street like an extra in a low-budget
zombie movie, dragging along herky-jerkily and possibly
emitting a gentle moan.

The next thing I remember is lying on top of my bed,
watching the light come up in the other room through a half-
opened door. I was still wearing my down coat, and a faint
revulsion rose with the realization that there was outerwear in
contact with the bed; at least I was still on top of the duvet,
not touching the sheets. But I didn't move, or couldn't. Things
like outside clothes seemed not to matter in the in-between,
if that's what this strange limbo was. I think the cat was there.
I must have fed him—or my body had—because everything
was blessedly quiet.

Hours passed and I don't remember moving. I think I must

have slept; at that point it may not have mattered if I was asleep or awake. I do remember feeling like this was correct somehow; this was where I was always meant to be, nowhere.

Hours passed.

I awoke to Swinton's substantial orange bulk on my chest, purring. I was still on the bed zipped into my coat. I was confused—what had happened? Had I done all the tasks I'd set myself that night—was it last night, the night before? I'd read somewhere that when you die, your cat will only eat the soft parts of your face. My soft parts seemed still to be intact. I looked into Swinton's solemn gold-green eyes and wondered what he was plotting. And all of a sudden, I was afraid—not of him or for him exactly, but of myself—a feeling I could not remember having before. Something told me that I could not stay in the in-between forever. I needed to go one way or the other. I had been so sure but now I didn't know what to do. I made a sound—I remember the feeling in my throat so clearly, a keening wail ripping out of me like it was tearing off skin as it went—and the cat leapt away, his claws digging into my coat as he pushed off.

I called a friend to help me decide: Abigail, a psychiatrist, who'd wisely been planting seeds for months about how the hospital was just a place "to rest." I remember thinking that it would give me more time to make a clearheaded decision about how to leave the in-between, whether to live or die. That is why I went to the hospital.

You know what happened then. Time passed, I did not read, I did not know that I was living.

After that long night and long day and the hospital and after my return to Oxford to convalesce with Merve's family, I found myself at home in New York, alone once more with the reproachful cat and my equally reproachful books. They both seemed upset by my prolonged absence. I had just started reading again, released from acute bibliophobia by Helen DeWitt, but that didn't mean I knew how to shake off its chronic effects. I knew I had to keep reading, and I knew that soon enough, I would have to start writing again. That seemed impossible.

So, I started the only place I knew how. When I write about a book, I need to copy out every phrase or passage that speaks to me. It takes hours or days to do this painstaking reread, but this copying feels like meditation or prayer, and without it I don't think I could write new words at all. I've been doing this for so many years that now, I'm afraid I cannot know anything about a text, much less write anything about it, if I have not mimed the act of its inscription myself. Uncertain that I would ever think original thoughts again, much less write them, I started by taking *The Last Samurai* down from the shelf. I opened it and began typing.

*

I wish I could explain to you the very specific feeling of safety that enfolds me during this process. Copying can feel dully, predictably good. At best, it's a sensation completely different from the overexcited nausea I get from actually writing. Copying out a text is like a predictable small luxury, like waking up on a long weekend's Monday and lingering guiltlessly in pleasant half sleep for an extra hour. Sometimes in these reveries I feel like I could do it all day, for days on end, for the rest of my life.

Sometimes I think about Flaubert's exquisite idiots Bouvard and Pécuchet, the subjects of his unfinished last novel, two copy clerks who retire to the countryside determined to explore the depth and breadth of human knowledge, only to give up and return to their jobs copying documents till the end of their days. I envy them on occasion. But I know I couldn't really be happy like that. And, try though I may to just type and not think, more often than not, my copying is not just rote replication. As I retype the words, a new kind of participatory rereading comes into play; somehow knowing what is going to happen in a novel and reinscribing it feels like *making* the events happen. I slide into a peculiar limbo, between myself and the text itself. Sometimes, when copying out a passage that I experience keenly—so keenly that I could be writing it myself for the first time, not reading it for the second or third or tenth time—there is a confusing slippage.*

I can never figure out if all writers feel this way, or if it's just me, and if so, what that might mean. When I am copying out a passage, at times I feel as though I am coming to these words on my own. I can forget that they are already on the page beside me, and I'm just transcribing them. I feel like

---

* For years, I have not been able to escape Jorge Luis Borges's short story "Pierre Menard, Author of the *Quixote*." Menard is a fellow copyist who is not a copyist. His lifelong mission is to spontaneously produce *Don Quixote* in exactly the same words as Cervantes, without referring to the text—but with different meaning. The desired coincidence—the *coincide*-ence—of Cervantes's *Quixote* and Menard's *Quixote* delights and unsettles me. What I experience is some version of this: When I'm copying certain texts, at times it does feel like I am not just retyping their printed words, but that I am somehow making them anew, transforming them through repetition without visible difference. Right now, reading "Pierre Menard" for the nth time and typing lines of it into my notes for this essay, I suspect that I myself am in fact authoring Borges authoring Menard authoring Cervantes.

some batty Victorian spiritualist doing automatic writing,
channeling something from the ether to the page. It sometimes happens that I'll be typing out a phrase, then a sentence,
then find myself just continuing to type out the whole paragraph, or even the whole page. There are books in which I've
gotten completely lost, lulled into a kind of possessed fugue,
such that I could very well go and retype the whole thing. This
is an exhilarating feeling because the text lulls me into this
wholly incarnate reading experience—what Borges, channeling Novalis, calls "a *total* identification with a given author."
But it's also a sinking one because, as I type further and further, I come to understand that this author has already written, in the very words that I would use, the very book that I
am trying to write. Maybe this really is automatic writing of a
sort, but somehow I realize that the book was the living thing
all along. I see that I am only a ghost haunting the text itself,
not the medium being haunted.

The should be the best feeling, encountering the books
that say just what you want to say. This is the dream of the
searching reader: to find that impossible text that fully understands you, seems to know your mind better than you do,
reads your soul and recites it back to you, challenging you to
examine its flaws. I have been lucky; I have met many of these
books over the years. Yet the longer I try to write about books,
the more that companionship has turned tense. Finding a
book like this now, I rarely feel anything more positive than a
queasy swirl of excitement and dread.

The great cruelty of writing is this realization that the experience for which I long the most as a reader—an encounter
with someone who makes me believe that they have articu-
lated exactly my thoughts, exactly my feelings, in the most

perfect and irreplaceable terms—is a kind of death. The sublimity of total recognition is the sublimity of inescapable failure; reading the text you have been searching for means that
you can never write it. Discovering something like this is to
experience at once a thrilling and a hopeless self-obliteration.

*

Sitting at my desk, staring down a document beginning to
creep onto its twelfth page of single-spaced lines from DeWitt
(DeWitticisms?) I wondered what else there was to write. I
could not go back to my monograph, not yet, maybe not ever.
All I could think about or remember was what just happened:
the hospital, the aftermath. So I tried to do as Geoff Dyer did,
and get "*interested in depression.*" Until then, memoirs of mental illness had not appealed to me; even now, after reading
many of them, I find the genre difficult to face. After encountering Elizabeth Wurtzel's *Prozac Nation* in college and feeling affronted by both how like and how utterly unlike it was
to my experience of adolescence, I wholly avoided books of
this type. I told myself snootily that it was because I found the
genre of memoir on the whole distasteful. But, preparing to
start this project, I came to realize that I had actually been
afraid of reading other writers' depression books. Afraid, in a
general sense, of finding myself replicated too precisely in
other accounts of writers having breakdowns. And more specifically, afraid that I would get dangerously lost in the text
and find myself becoming less and less like a person writing a
new book—and less and less like a person at all.

Confronted with this fear, I started my research with a
clinical account, the American Psychiatric Association's *Di-*

agnostic and Statistical Manual of Mental Disorders, fifth edition, better known as the *DSM.* This looked safe to me. The
neutral tones of the reference book seemed like just the right
tonic for my concerns about losing myself to the text; I found
it highly unlikely that I would get lulled into copying out nine
hundred pages of psychiatric diagnostic criteria that were
themselves famously limited. I'd been given official diagnoses
during my stay in the hospital, and now I felt, for the first
time, an avid interest in what those diagnoses had to say for
themselves. Overall, I'd found them somewhat unimpressive
at the time, even a little disappointingly obvious and blasé:
major depressive disorder, obsessive-compulsive disorder, bu-
limia nervosa. I didn't know what everyone else's diagnoses
were, but I felt shamefully that they must be more serious
than mine.

It was like grad school all over again. Almost everyone else
on the ward had a yellow bracelet signifying that they'd been
undergoing shock therapy; everyone else had meaningful and
significant problems that could be classified as genuine illness. I was just an imposter who'd overindulged in self-pity
and accidentally landed myself in the ER. After all, most of
my friends since college had, at some point, considered themselves at least a little depressed, at least a little OCD, and, in
the case of the majority of my female friends, at least dabblers
in disordered eating. Here I was again, I thought, *copying.* Assimilating. And worse, assimilating badly. If I alone of all the
people I knew had ended up in psychiatric care, it must have
been through some weakness or additional flaw of my own.
My family, like many other non-Americans of various kinds,
didn't really believe in the concept of mental health, and I felt
a familiar tickle of insufficiency. I'd been resisting a break-

down for so long partly because I didn't believe in my right to have it, as someone who was not, as my father would have delicately put it, "really insane." My diagnoses, which looked so harmless compared to so many other possible diagnoses, just didn't seem like enough to justify the damage I'd selfishly invited into my life, and the lives of those close to me.

Reading the *DSM*, though, I felt strangely emboldened, and through that emboldening, oddly embodied. It was the opposite of the ghostliness I'd been afraid of. The text *did* tell me, in unvarnished, inelegant prose, much of what I thought and felt and did; it turns out that I am a textbook case. Despite the intellectual skepticism I knew I was supposed to retain toward the *DSM*, I found myself nodding along with the reading, like a song I'd known for years, whose lyrics I could never forget. Certain lines, often the least dramatic ones, really struck me as touchingly correct. "Sadness may be denied at first but may be elicited through interview or inferred from facial expression and demeanor"—the dry obviousness of this observation both made me laugh out loud and feel a pang of surprising tenderness toward both the imagined doctor and patient. Seeing so many of the thoughts and behaviors I had assumed were universal defined explicitly as abnormal was reassuring and weirdly pleasurable; I felt a peculiar pride in recognizing some of my habits that was not unlike the thrill of finding unexpected, candid pictures of yourself in a high school yearbook—maybe not the most flattering ones, but images where you look startlingly just like yourself.

This simplistic likeness felt completely different from the blurring of self that I'd feared. For some reason, seeing my behavior sketched in such confident, clinical lines made me feel more, rather than less, real; I felt comfortingly anonymous, just one officially depressed person suddenly made legible by my enrollment in an unseen international association of other officially depressed people. Reading the facts of my life so plainly in the medical text, I experienced a certain kind of identification, but not of the type conventionally associated with literary reading. Rather, it was the specific, snug pigeonhole of a fitting diagnosis. As Esmé Weijun Wang writes, "a diagnosis is comforting because it provides a framework—a community, a lineage—and, if luck is afoot, a treatment or cure." I like her use of the word "lineage," which suggests the intimate affiliation of illness, stretching back into time and across the globe; my usual, tired sense of small-scale familial estrangement gives way to a timid feeling of belonging to a great transhistorical family of declared melancholics. "Lineage" speaks to the vague reassurance of family resemblance, a kind, homely feeling. I was not special, the *DSM* told me, nor did I have to be special in order to be officially fucked up, and that realization was an incredible relief.

Braced by the blunt assertiveness of the *DSM,* I felt ready to tackle the growing stack of depression books beside my desk. I sped through the classics of the genre, lingering especially on accounts of scholarly depression like Julia Kristeva's *Black Sun,* William Styron's *Darkness Visible,* and Kay Redfield Jamison's *An Unquiet Mind.* I reencountered *Prozac Nation* and found it even more affronting than the last time, then got mired for a while in Andrew Solomon's fascinating and intimidatingly comprehensive study *The Noonday Demon.* I enjoyed some of these books and abandoned others partway through; none of them troubled any deep well of feeling within me as I leafed through them day by day, through the weeks of spring and summer.

But then I started a book that shook me right back out of
my body, back into nothingness and spectrality. I started reading it on a Wednesday, right after therapy. I'd just been telling
my therapist that I wanted, in some part of this book, to explain how I interact with literary characters. Thinking about
these fears of absorption, I'd realized that I hardly ever *identify* with characters. Part of the reason the Carson experiment
had felt so exceptional was the immediate and unfamiliar way
I fell into willing alignment with the speaker herself (and just
as quickly and wholly out of it). In general, when my students
speak positively about a character being "relatable," I always
have to repress an irritated, perhaps jealous sigh. I had a vague
memory of feeling like that about specific characters, once
upon a time, but I could no longer remember which ones I'd
related to in what books, or why. I'd begun to worry that this
lack of relation meant that I myself was not relatable, not legible or distinguishable in the scheme of known human feeling. The alarming sensation that I've been trying to describe,
of haunting a text or letting it haunt me, is not about inhabiting a character. Instead, I experience these moments of
getting pulled into a text as a frightening total convergence
between my self—whatever immaterial thing that is—and
the text as a whole. I tried to explain this to my therapist, but
she presented me with that placid, carefully blank therapist
face, the one they seem to learn for those moments when a
patient just spouts absolute nonsense. "We'll continue with
this next week," she said.

I slowly walked home to begin the next book in my depression stack, Yiyun Li's *Dear Friend, from My Life I Write to You
in Your Life*. I'd felt some trepidation approaching this one. I
liked the cover, a blotted blur of sea colors that looked like a

cloud or a spill, and I loved the title—it was the kind of title I found myself wanting to say out loud all the time, the way a teenager can't help but say the name of her crush too often. I had a feeling that this book would speak to me, and I wanted to listen, but I was afraid. This intuition of affinity—it made me nervous.

Nervousness became half-pleasurable, half-anxious fear as I read. I know that Yiyun Li and I have very little in common. We share an absurdly generalized racial category and, at the time, we shared an employer. We are both writers, though she is, in my mind, a Writer with a capital *W* and I am not. We have both been in psychiatric hospitals. But that's about it. I know that I am not actually her ghost; I understood that we were both technically alive in the world in the year 2019. Yet, reading Li's book, I felt myself start to fade and become spectral. I felt that the book knew more than I could know about myself; even though the events of our lives are so different, I feared that it had gotten to all my thoughts before I had a chance to think them.

This is not identification. Identification, as I've observed it in friends and students, can be an assertion of selfness through sympathetic attachment. The reader can see their own feelings and inclinations (or those they wish they possessed) in a character, and paradoxically, through latching on to that character, practices some version of autonomy and self-knowledge. What I experienced reading *Dear Friend* was something more like identification's antithesis, in which, seeing my own thoughts and feelings replicated so precisely on the page, I began to doubt whether those thoughts and feelings were ever mine in the first place. I felt my mind undone by my encounter with the text. Parts of me sank into the typed words and others dissipated in the white spaces in between those letters and symbols. I became invisible to myself. Li herself says this better than I can: "I did not see myself in Scarlett O'Hara," she writes, "or Anna Karenina or Tess Durbeyfield or Jane Eyre; nor did I look for myself in Jean-Christophe or Nick Adams or Paul Morel or the old man fighting the sea. To read oneself into another person's tale is the opposite of how and why I read. To read is to be with people who, unlike those around one, do not notice one's existence."

Reading Li's memoir of depression, suicidality, reading, and writing, I started to lose track of myself. My thoughts and hers would come together in discombobulating unison, then split into a strange harmony that took me over completely. Li writes that she reads with the express purpose of becoming invisible; after years of doing this too, I am alarmed by the frequency with which invisibility comes upon me unintentionally. Reading a book that felt so much like myself made me wonder if it—the book—was the *real* me, and I only its shade.

The funny thing about my fellow feeling with this particular quote is that in it, Li expresses her lack of identification, which is precisely what, for lack of a better word, I identify with. This is something of a philosophical problem. What does it mean to relate to someone's lack of relation? What relationship does that then put me into with Li, if we are both invisible figures haunting the books we read? If she was a ghost, was I just a ghost of a ghost? I cringed with both fear and shame.

This shame is not unrelated to the way I think about suicide. As Li writes, "People who have not experienced a suicidal urge miss a crucial point. It is not that one wants to end one's life,

but that the only way to end the pain—that eternal fight against
one's melodrama so that it does not transgress—is to wipe out
the body." The "melodrama"—THE MELODRAMA!—is exactly it. This phrase reminds me that I have often wondered if
someday I will simply be mortified into killing myself, after so
many failed attempts. That word, "mortification," is one of my
favorites. These days, we almost always use it to signify great
embarrassment, and forget its original meaning of "to deaden"
or "put to death." It reminds me of a moment I love at the end
of the Balzac novella *Adieu!:* The narrator's love object, driven
mad by historical trauma, doesn't just die like a normal person.
Rather, faced finally with the end of the tragic, unfinished love
story she's been reliving for many years, she "corpsifies herself"
("elle se corpsifie"). It's more sublime than tragic in Balzac's use,
but more comic than sublime when I imagine what it would
mean for me. To corpsify myself: Surely that would be the ulti-
mate stage of mortification, to be flat-out *embarrassed to death*
by the melodrama of my stupid little life, my ridiculous, insub-
stantial problems with books.

*

One of the things I admire most about Li's book is how
matter-of-factly she uses the word "suicide." None of my
friends ever say the word "suicide." Only Merve even addresses it directly, though she never uses the *s*-word, when
once every month or two, she asks if I still feel like killing
myself. This sounds harsh, but it's an implicitly agreed-upon
check-in between the two of us; brusque, necessary, even laced
with the humor of the quotidian. (Don't worry, I tell her these
days. My skincare regimen proves that I want to live. If I ever

stop exfoliating again, you can be alarmed.) But nobody else has used those words. I'm interested in Li's account of talking to people she knows about suicide. She relates the words that people have used to dissuade her: "a suicide attempt is selfish. Someone close to me said it was irresponsible; another said manipulative. Yes, I know what you mean, I said to each of them."

This is a part of the book that I have not yet lived because I have not yet had these conversations with the people I know. I wonder if the conversations Li related are premonitions of the ones I will have to have. I'm not sure if my friends don't use this language with me because they are too squeamish or because they just don't want to take me back to it. I'm also just not sure what they know; I can't account for what I've told them about why I went to the hospital, or what had happened to me the other times. I wonder if they would use those same words if we were ever to talk about it, those loving condemnations. I've always assumed that they would, which is perhaps why I let things remain veiled and politely oblique. Instead of saying "I tried to kill myself," I say, "I went to the hospital," and instead of saying "Please don't die," they say things like "What can I do" or "I'm sorry, I didn't know." I don't want to introduce this blunter language because I'm afraid it would hurt them.

But personally, I have never been afraid of the word "suicide," or the act it names, perhaps because I have never been afraid of dying. It seems ridiculous to say so, but I whimsically suspect this is because, living as I have among books, I have been cultivating the feeling of being a ghost for a long time. It's not exactly a bad thing. That's the feeling I've been trying to describe here: the sublime self-destruction of burying yourself in a book, haunting it and being haunted by it. Thinking back to "The Unquiet Grave," I'm reminded that suicides were historically buried in unhallowed ground, often a crossroads. I think again of the moment with the Child Ballads in the basement stacks, late at night, surrounded by books terrifyingly more alive than me, or of Smith's narrator, facing the ghost amid their shared bookshelves. Writing this, I'm realizing that the library is its own kind of unhallowed ground, fathoms deep and dense with stories and their ghosts—of which I am only one. This is a terrifying feeling, but also one I have taken comfort in many times.

I have to laugh. It's hilarious to think that the most trivial and quotidian of life's troubles can be summed up in the same words as the most deep and metaphysical ones: How do you go on after you've been ghosted? Seriously, though. For so long I have thought of myself as some other writer's ghost—but maybe that's just an easy way out, a way to avoid really looking directly at the story I am always in the middle of both reading and writing.

Perhaps I have only ever been my own ghost, my own spectral reader. If that's true, by finally writing my own book, can I summon myself back to life?

Chapter 8

THE LAST CHAPTER

Once upon a time, I truly believed that there *was* a book that could have saved me; I might half-melodramatically, half-seriously say that it was also the book that almost killed me. The book you're reading now is haunted by it—the ghost of a book I never finished. This book-that-never-was is my dissertation, the long work of literary criticism I had to produce in order to get a PhD and my academic job. In order to get tenure, I would have had to revise and polish the dissertation book for publication at a prestigious academic press. By the time my department's decision finally came in 2021, I still hadn't published it, so I didn't get tenure—a fancy way of saying I got fired. I could tell myself and my friends that I had made a willful choice simply not to do it and that I had never been cut out for academia anyway. But in my heart, I really believed that it was because I was simply too stupid and too weak to take the pressure. If I had just been better, I would have saved the book, and it would have saved my career—

saved *me*. It still takes a great effort not to look back at the last decade and a half of my life and feel this way.

When I can successfully fight off this feeling, it is very clear to me that for much of that time, I was debilitated by depression—for years, not just the few short months of my hospital stay and medical leave of absence. Before and after the breakdown, I was consumed by the belief that tenure and the lifetime of job security it offered were the only things that could possibly matter. After the hospital, even though I talked with my therapist every week about how I needed to let go of this single overweening goal to move on, it actually seemed even more urgent. Around that time, I became obsessed with the idea that, no matter how much better I felt, a day would come when I'd have to be admitted to the hospital again. In group therapy, I had been the only first-timer, and everyone else talked about how afraid they were that if they got out, they'd just be back in the unit again in a month or a year. I believed that I couldn't afford to lose my job and my insurance because that next period of madness could fall upon me at any time. Desperately, I chiseled away at the book right up until the tenure decision, taking parts away and adding parts on, vainly hoping that there might be untapped life in it. Looking back, I think of it like Frankenstein's creature, whom the naïve scientist adorns with pearly white teeth and glistening black hair, thinking that these ornamental bits and bobs can make the whole beautiful. I don't think I've ever hated and loved something in such equal measure.

I had the unsettling experience recently of looking back at this book, which felt a bit like attending a wake—or more accurately, a clinical viewing of the body. It was a strange feeling—the book was definitely dead, but I could still hear the whisperings of the life it once had, or could have had. I was astounded to see that it was very long and not all bad. The thing whispering to me, I thought, was the ghost of a better, stronger Sarah-that-never-was, one who published the book, got tenure, did what she was supposed to do, did not let herself get inconveniently derailed by mental illness. It spoke to me smugly like Pecola's mirror image in *The Bluest Eye*, taunting me: "You're just jealous." As if that life could ever have been real. As if it had been a choice.

This book, which could perhaps have saved my academic life, was about a concept I called "denarrative desire." The phrase is a play on two well-established terms in narrative theory. The "de-" in denarrative desire comes from a backwards-running impulse, one that implicitly rejects the finality of endings. Basically, the denarrating narrator attempts to take back what has already been said; as narrative theorist Brian Richardson explains, "The simplest example of this might be something like, 'Yesterday it was raining. Yesterday it was not raining.'"

The "desire" part comes from the psychoanalytic literary critic Peter Brooks's 1984 book, *Reading for the Plot*, in which he proposes that readers are driven to read by "narrative desire," which is a kind of Freudian death drive. We know that our pleasure in the book and the lives we're living through it will end at the last page, but we are compelled to move forward anyway, driven by the certainty that the only thing that ultimately bestows meaning and resonance upon a narrative is closure—the death knell of "The End."

Altogether, denarrative desire is basically the idea that sometimes, when you reach the end of a book, all you want to do is turn back to the first page and read it over again—but *differently.**

The book would always end the same way, no matter how many times you reread it, or hoped in vain that it would turn

---

*   As I wrote long ago in this nonbook's introduction:

> This project began with a simple speculation: if narrative desire is our end-seeking death drive, then what are we to make of the feeling of loss and abandonment that we find in the blank abyss that follows, the vacant non-afterlife of a desired next page that never comes? One answer immediately presents itself: we turn back to the source of the story; we return to Page 1. The dissatisfaction of reading is incurable, but one might try and assuage it by *rereading*—finding, once we've fulfilled our drive to get to the end of a story, that it provokes a perverse, equal and opposite desire to go back to the beginning. In keeping with the contrarian nature of this impulse, I began to think of this Newtonian narrative backlash as *denarrative desire:* namely, the inexorable yearning to turn the pages back and read them, or, more dramatically, to *write them* again.
>
> Yet the problem of rewriting is the writer's (and reader's) recognition of the impossibility of unwriting. For rewriting implies rereading, and any act of retelling or reshaping cannot actually erase the original text that lurks beneath and within a new incarnation. . . . Denarrative desire turns the pages back, inserting new pages to render other narrative possibilities visible (while covering up the ones that we are unhappy with). But *writing over* is not the same as erasing; generating more narrative never actually undoes that first reading. Despite the urgent want to re-view—to see something else from a different angle—you can't unsee something, just as you can't unwrite what is written, or make someone unread what they have already read. The originary death still lurks in the text, regardless of how it is reread or reconfigured; in Brooks' words, "Once there is text, expression, writing, one becomes subject to the processes of desiring and dying."

I cannot express the perverse pleasure it gives me to consign this book that took so much of my life to a footnote.

out differently. As for books, so too for life. I was obsessed then with novels that attempt to rewrite historical narratives knowing that they must fail, books that rewrite earlier books like Jean Rhys's *Wide Sargasso Sea* rewrites *Jane Eyre* knowing all the while what Brontë wrote must come to pass—and books that rewrite *themselves* as they're happening, seeking a happier ending, like Kate Atkinson's *Life After Life*. Books that play upon the reader's yearning hope that more meaning can be extracted or even produced after the supposed end of a story. This much I knew; this much I was comfortable announcing to colleagues and friends and myself. But what I couldn't allow myself to see, or to say, was that this was just another expression of my own fixation on "The End." The whole time I was planning, writing, and revising that unfinished book, I was still so certain that there was only one way for my story to end, eventually: in suicide. The last chapter had been prewritten. And after that end, I hoped, everything that had happened or not happened in my life could finally make some kind of perverse narrative sense to the people I loved—my "readers"—if they went back and reread the text of my short life. The inevitability of the end helped me get through the everyday.

In a horribly irresponsible way, it let me off the hook. I was consumed with the idea—which I now recognize as willfully stupid and cruelly selfish—that this clear ending would force everyone to see that there was no other way for the story to end, and therefore that none of the other characters in it—themselves included—could have stopped the forward motion of the plot or revised the final page. As the philosopher Simon Critchley writes in his *Notes on Suicide*, "Suicide produces a peculiar inversion of biography, where all of one's acts are read backwards through the lens of one's last moment." Read through my death, I was sure that my life's trajectory would eventually make sense to everyone else, if not to me.

If I'm being totally honest, it's the only thing I feel truly *bad* about, looking back at this whole period. The idea that killing myself would offer any kind of firm narrative closure, and therefore an opportunity for interpretation, as though my friends would look back through that lens and see clearly and analytically that there was nothing anyone could have done, is not just stupid—it's madness. The fact that I could only think of myself as a text and my friends as readers in an enclosed, safe network of narrative theoretical concepts—that is also madness. There are many ways in which I've tried to rationalize and analyze the other aspects of my illness, but this is one thing I cannot make any sense of. But I really, earnestly believed that it was true, and that it would be better for everyone if I just hurried up and did it. The sooner I forced this ending, I thought, the sooner everyone could just get over it. There were other, better books out there for them to read.

This is the measure of how far outside reality I was in those years. It was only long after the hospital, and after the slow realization that I had to let go of my stagnant, stubborn reading of the text of my own life to parse it clearly, that I saw how wildly irrational this belief was. Its foolishness, and its cruelty, was made clear to me in starkest relief by *The Guardians: An Elegy for a Friend,* Sarah Manguso's account of grieving her friend Harris, who committed suicide by jumping in front of a train. It is a short, terribly beautiful and loving book. "It doesn't matter if he thought of me, wanted to call me, missed me, felt angry at me, loved me," Manguso writes, "but it's impossible not to invite oneself into the black box of a forsaken mind." Of course, it is impossible to keep people from rereading and rereading and rereading a life that ends in this kind of violence, wondering if they could have been more supportive secondary characters, and to torture themselves wondering if they could have done anything—*anything*—to change the plot. How could I not have understood this? How could I not have known better?

*

I was more and more fixated on the idea of life as narrative structure, and narrative structure as control. Both my belief in the immovable genre of my life—the suicide plot—and my belief in the fantastical possibility of being saved by the right book—the reading plot—were further enabled by the idea that I myself had become nothing but a text. It felt so important to be able to give a clear account of what was happening in it—to show up to a meeting with a colleague, or a drinks date with a friend, ready to deliver a neatly organized book report. I alternated between being someone who was forever at the mercy of plots I had no control over, and being someone who believed they knew exactly how those plots worked: in other words, between being a character and being a critic. Nowhere did I take responsibility for being my own author.

Until the breakdown happened. The real shock was not that it finally arrived, but that there was something on the other side. Over the years leading up to it, I'd been so sure that the next acute crisis would be the last. When the time came, and I asked for help, nobody was more shocked than I. It was like I'd turned to the end of a book I'd read a hundred times and found that somehow the words had changed—or rather, that I myself had unwittingly rewritten them. My denarrative desire had been fulfilled. Rather than being delighted by this transformation, I was at a loss. Despite the fact that I had never pitched it, it seemed that a sequel had been greenlit. The end was not the end.

Neither of the plots I'd been following diligently in my life to this point had come to their proper conclusions: I had not killed myself, and it had not been a book that saved me. It was in this discombobulated state that my most intense period of bibliophobia began, those months after the hospital when I could not make sense of the written word, and could not even start to read a book, much less finish writing one. I cannot deny that this reaction was probably chemical; I was on a new medication that was wreaking havoc with the way I thought, ate, and slept, so it seems obvious that it would wreak havoc with that other essential bodily function, reading. But I am convinced that it also had to do with the fact that both of those competing tenets of faith that I'd been upholding and secretly cultivating for my whole life had been torn down. Neither the creation nor apocalypse myths that I'd believed in so fervently had come to pass. I was, for the first time, without a sacred text to rely upon. I understood for the first time what it meant to lose one's faith, and to be relieved, but also terrified of entering the unknowable territory outside the enclosure of belief, which suddenly seems so small, so insufficient.

In the spring of 2019, when I went back to Oxford to stay with Merve and the family, and "rest," or whatever it is privileged people are supposed to do to live gently and harmlessly after they lose their minds, I was confused. The return to the place where the breakdown had started was strange, like a weird do-over, or like rereading the book of my life yet another time. Again, I was in Oxford after a dramatic event—not a breakup but a breakdown—and again, I was supposed to be recovering and working productively on my book at the same time; even though I was on medical leave, I still heard the tenure clock ticking. Merve's children, too, were like living clocks, who showed in the newly British shapes of their vowels how many months had passed since I'd greeted them there the last summer. The older of them, who was born at the very beginning of my long period of depression, made me realize just how many years I had lost to this round of illness—so long that he had become this odd, tiny person, who would sternly call me to order if I was too slow to find a puzzle piece ("Aunt Sarah, pay *attention!*") and seemed in moments more like a very short adult than the baby I still thought of him as. This was not a repetition; this was something new.

I've already told you about the book that allowed me—or maybe invited me, or maybe *forced* me—to read again, Helen DeWitt's *The Last Samurai*. I kept thinking for months and months about how the book wrought this change. I knew it had something to do with the need to reinvent my own reading practices, but there was something else. This year, I read it again. I thought maybe whatever had made this book open up to me had to do with the failure of language; after all, Ludo and Sibylla are always trying to learn new languages and are never satisfied with the limits of what they can communicate. I felt this frustration, but that was not it. I read it again. Then I thought it was Kurosawa, maybe; I watched and rewatched

Seven Samurai, and, despite the therapeutic epiphany that I have always seen too much of my father in Toshiro Mifune's character, that didn't seem to be it, either. I read it again.

The fourth time, I noticed something I had not noticed before. Ludo, a fatherless boy, has been scouring London for a surrogate father. But he is also searching for some way to save Sibylla (his mother) from her worsening depression— a depression depicted so undramatically, in the periphery and not the center of the book, and with such wry matter-of-factness that it created a knot, not of sympathy but of familiarity, in my stomach that twisted tighter and tighter with every reread. It was suddenly so clear—or rather, it had been *too* clear all along and I had been trying to run away from that clarity this whole time. Despite the fact that she narrates half of the book, Sibylla remains somehow just *too* showily on the sidelines; Ludo is the boy genius, the "Infant Terrible," the prodigious wonder, and it seemed on readings one through three that it ends up being *his* book. This last reading made me own up to something that had been so glaringly obvious that I hadn't wanted to admit it—I, who always prided myself on finding the least obvious reading, the one no one else would look for.

I *identified* with Sibylla.

As is stupidly so often true, it was so hard to admit the most evident thing. I saw myself in her more and more, whether I wanted to or not (the truth is, I both wanted to *and* not). In this last reading, there were moments when I found myself uncannily aligned with her; at the beginning of the book she describes herself sitting in the Upper Reading Room of the Radcliffe Camera in Oxford, just where I had sat during my Carson month, "looking out across a bell of air," distracted from the scholarly task (a translation from German) she's there to accomplish. I realized that there were moments and lines I'd fixed on as "important" or "meaningful"—"a good samurai will parry the blow"—that come from Ludo. But the moments that hit me the hardest, right in the gut, the moments that seemed so facilely self-evident or too frighteningly understandable almost all belonged to Sibylla.

Midway through the novel, frustrated by his search for a father, Ludo asks Sib if she ever considered an abortion when she was pregnant with him. It was very late, she tells him, and the counselor she spoke to recommended adoption. But, she says to them, "how could I be sure your adoptive parents would teach you how to leave life if you did not care for it & they said What and I said—well you know I said what any rational person would say . . ."

Obviously, I had thought on my first reading in Oxford, and my second and third readings back home later. The only thing a rational person would say.

It was only on this fourth reading that I finally saw that the book's bells and whistles—Ludo's charm and accomplishments and the novel's formal card tricks and Sibylla's own philological hand-waving—had been a welcome distraction. I'd been looking for the reason this novel spoke so urgently to me—that first time and all the subsequent ones—but trying to find answers in all the wrong places. It was Sibylla who spoke to me—asking the questions that I had been asking for so long and never finding a sufficient answer. I didn't just have to relearn how to read in order to find hidden truths or new revelations. I had to relearn how to read in order to see what was already there, what was in the text all along that I had allowed myself not to see, not to dwell on.

Near the end of his quest, Ludo has an encounter with Red
Devlin, the only one of his father candidates who does not
disappoint him, that is one of the most moving and gener-
ously undramatic depictions of suicide ever committed to the
page. Ludo interrupts Devlin, a journalist who has witnessed
and experienced too much cruelty in the world to continue
living, as he is preparing to take an overdose of pills. The conversation they have is sad, wretchedly absurd, and wretchedly
real, and ends—quietly, humanely—with Devlin's death. At
one point, Ludo narrates a phone call Sibylla once made to
the Samaritans, the British suicide helpline:

> My mother, I said, called the Samaritans once and
> asked whether research had been done on thwarted
> suicides to find out whether they had spent the time
> after the incident happily.
> What did they say?
> They said they didn't know.
> He grinned.

This was it. This was what had changed things for me—this
admission of simply not knowing what came after, not knowing how to continue living. These exact words came at the end
of the book, but the idea was written into it from the beginning. *The Last Samurai* is not a book that tries to make sense
of life. It is a book that seeks answers but knows that explana-
tions are impossible—and to attempt to give them, as Sibylla
does to many a nonplussed stranger, only leads to frustration.
And in that moment, not knowing how to move on and no
longer even knowing how to start to find out, I needed a text
that met me where I was: at a point where it was painfully

clear that books and stories are not enough. And yet, it was equally clear that their very insufficiencies—the moments at which they strain to meet our depths of confusion and despair and perhaps acknowledge their own failures—are sometimes exactly what we need.

YARROW STALKS

Since my narrative failed to end how I thought it would, I have thought a lot about what it means to have the stories that you tell yourself, about yourself, suddenly revised. In recent months, my response has been to develop an irritating habit. Whenever I start to shape real-life events into a good story, I stop myself short. No doubt, this makes conversing with me a chaotic experience. The private stories I used to rely on—the plot of my death and the plot of the magical book that could save me from it—are no longer ones that I count on. The narrative arc of my academic career is complete; I am no longer a professor and no longer on the path to any permanent state of professional being. Depression is still part of my life, and it will always be; I cannot say if there will be another chapter in that story, when it might begin, or if it will ever end.

That not-knowing is the hardest thing to accept, but also the most necessary. I recently read Donald Antrim's *One Friday in April*, subtitled "A Story of Suicide and Survival." I knew this book existed and had made a note of it when it was published. But I had forgotten about it, or made myself forget. I read it in a couple of hours lying flat on the couch and only got up three times, once to pee and twice to move my agitated body around unsteadily, alternately crouching and pacing. The rest of the time, I just lay there, tears sliding down my face and soaking the pillow beneath me like a sour, damp halo, and turning pages, occasionally keening so loud and tragicomically that I wondered, as I often do, what the employees of the concrete company downstairs must have thought.

The first time I had to pause and walk it off was when Antrim describes a call he received in the middle of a monthslong stay at the New York State Psychiatric Institute. The call was from David Foster Wallace, who he did not know, but with whom he shared a mutual friend. This friend had told DFW about Antrim's situation, and Wallace called to gently urge the sick man to consent to electroconvulsive therapy. Antrim's fears about ECT are my own: "I knew," he writes, "or thought I knew, what shock would do to me. It would destroy my ability to write, or even to think clearly. It would take away my memories and my personality. I would be unable to function, and live confined to hospital wards." I too was afraid of ECT for these exact reasons in the hospital. Wallace called Antrim to tell him that ECT was safe and helpful and to convince him to try it. "Tell me one more time?" Antrim asks. Wallace does, and stays on the phone with Antrim, this man who is not his friend, but who needs his help and reassurance.

The thing that got me was not the ECT, or Antrim's fears that were so like my own, or Wallace's undramatic kindness, but the simple fact of his appearance and the knowledge that somewhere in the remaining fifty pages of the book, Antrim would have to recount the unavoidable fact of Wallace's suicide in 2008, less than two years after that phone call. I felt despair for Antrim, who had to write it in the book. I felt despair for Wallace, a writer I have only really felt connected to because of his depression and suicide (and his first novel's setting in Shaker Heights, Ohio, my first American home). And I felt despair for the idiotic optimism about being safe that I'd been allowing to take root, which in recent months had felt strong enough to grow on its own, without being constantly measured and fertilized. Wallace, I thought, was well enough to call Antrim and talk him calmly through this crisis, this crisis that he himself had experienced more than once. And still he did it. Still. He did it. To be confident in my ability to stay alive—to let myself grow confident and even complacent—suddenly felt foolhardy. I blushed with embarrassment as I quaked with sobs, a sharp heat subtly different from the fervid full-to-bursting feeling my face already had from crying nonstop for a couple of hours. "You fucking moron," I thought. "You idiot. How could you have been so stupid." It was not a question.

I have felt, since that winter and spring of 2019, like I might be different—not better, because that word is meaningless here, but further away, hidden skillfully from the immediate regard of death. In writing this book, I have often felt far, far away from the versions of myself who slowly and precisely carved at an inner arm or thigh with a paring knife or razor blade, or swallowed a bottle of pills; who stood looking down at the illogical swirl of waves under the Transmitter Park pier for hours, or swam way out alone at the beach and didn't care if I could get back. I have felt, at times, so far away from death that it is difficult to clearly summon up what it felt like in the hospital, or in the days before or after. Three years, I tell myself firmly, is a very long time. Yet there is so little distance in Antrim's book. It begins in medias res, "one Friday in April" in 2006. The writer is looking down from the roof of his four-story apartment building in Brooklyn, the building he still lives in now. He is not deciding whether or not to jump—decision doesn't enter into it. He is in a state of neither jumping nor not-jumping. He is in between. This must be, I recognize, a dramatic scene to most readers. Yet the title, which begins the first sentence of the book—"One Friday in April"—is so casual, almost airy in its familiarity. It is just one Friday in April like how the everlasting night before I went to the hospital was just one Saturday in February; just like every day when someone has tried or planned or succeeded at dying by suicide is just one random day in one random month, a random day that, to many of us, feels all too familiar.

I felt my whole body seize as I started reading the book; it did not relax until well after the last page. Not only because it feels so close to what I have felt over and over again through the years, in the world and in my apartment and in the hospital—but because of how close it seems to feel to Antrim still, a decade and a half later. He is able to recount the days and weeks and months of his hospital stays with such steady, flagellating precision. That doubled proximity makes me panic. All of a sudden, the attempts I've made to actively walk away or passively drift away from death seem so piddling. Three years is nothing. All of a sudden, I felt suicide looking at me again, and myself looking at it. I wonder what Antrim

felt, writing these lines. He describes a specific knife that has
meaning to him, an old Sabatier he took from his mother's
kitchen; I immediately, without thinking, pictured a specific
knife that has meaning to me, a small but unfailingly sharp
Shun knife that my brother gave me years ago, that I've held
against parts of my body many times, sometimes cutting,
sometimes not. Automatically, I felt a compulsion to go to the
kitchen drawer where it's sitting and take it out, just to hold
it. I could not stop myself—I did it. The cool flat of the blade
on the inside of my wrist felt like it always has, like a cold
compress on a fevered brow. I realized that these are not even
thoughts, but instincts that cannot be stopped because there
is no deciding moment in which to stop them. After all this
time and thinking, decision still doesn't enter into it. Once a
suicide, always a suicide, I thought, just like how someone
who's been sober for ten years is still an alcoholic. Three years
mean nothing at all.

The second moment that sent me into a breathless, floor-
crouching, couch-clutching panic came near the end of
Antrim's book. After the hospital, he says, "friends joked that
I was crazy, and I laughed along. Some suggested that a psychiatric history might enhance my literary reputation." I have
to wonder, horribly: Is this simply what I'm doing here, in this
book, trying to burnish my writerly credentials with this proof
that I've been through something real? Am I a fool to think
that I'm far away enough from it to write about it—am I still
not past it, but in it? A few pages later, he describes a moment
of "pretend[ing] my life was in order" and going off his meds.
Have I not also been trying to wean myself off my medications over the last year, telling my doctors and friends and

myself that we don't have to worry anymore? Am I not playing at health and wellness in the very act of writing this book,
in glibly regaling you with tales of my former troubles? Is it
not hubris or sheer stupidity to do any of this? After all, in
2010, after several years of something that most people would
call recovery, Antrim went back to the hospital, back for
thirty-seven more rounds of ECT. And if it happened to him,
why wouldn't it happen to me? If it happened to Wallace, why
wouldn't it happen to any of us?

There is no guarantee that it will not happen; I cannot in
good conscience tell you that I have totally let go of either the
suicide plot or the reading-for-salvation plot—for what is
this book if not a version of that? But these are no longer the
only possible outcomes. I am trying now to let life happen as
it happens, and to move through the world without construct-
ing a predetermined narrative to cling to. As a scholar and as
a book critic, my writing has mostly been about form; about
the form-making impulse in the work of different authors,
and the attraction narrative forms hold for us in our lives,
both in and out of books. In trying to let go of my own desire
to shape life into self-serving fictions, I have also had to re-
consider how I look at literary texts and at people. *Disinterest-
edness* is something I have become interested in, not as
dispassion or coldness, but rather as a way of receiving things
openly, without making demands of them.

But I am new at this, and there have been many moments
when I've found myself impatiently seeking out answers about
the plot of this new, unexpected volume of my life. A year ago,
as I was backsliding and freaking out about the unknowability
of the future, my friend Andrea saw me flailing and suggested

a distraction. It was a moment of specific, multiplied instability: waiting to hear if I would get a job, waiting to hear how bad the doctors thought my dad's newly diagnosed Alzheimer's was, waiting to see if a new relationship would work out. She offered to do an I Ching reading for me—all I had to do was ask a question. The one that came to mind was ridiculous, but it came out before I could help myself. When, I asked, would I know what was going to happen?

Andrea counted out the red yarrow stalks as I sat nervously, half-certain that it would not tell me anything, half-afraid that it would. Eventually she drew up the hexagram and flipped to the page about its meaning. The hexagram was *Hsü*—"Waiting."

We both burst out laughing. Of course, it served me right. For months, I had been going around telling everyone that I was no longer beholden to my own narrative-making impulses and that I was trying to cultivate a Zen cessation of desires. What did I expect if I asked the I Ching something that went so entirely against this goal? This was what I got for trying to play different Eastern mysticisms against each other. I felt appropriately trolled, like a monk who gets unceremoniously slapped by the abbot in some koan.

But then we read onward and realized that "Waiting" is not just the cosmic-comic insult we originally took it to be. We bent over the book companionably, slowly unfolding the meaning of the character together: "This hexagram shows the clouds in the heavens, giving rain to refresh all that grows and to provide mankind with food and drink. The rain will come in its own time. We cannot make it come; we have to wait for it."

Andrea looked at me with a half smile as she lifted a brow challengingly. "The rain will come in its own time."

I rolled my eyes at her, but felt a smile pull at my lips. I looked down at the next page, and my gaze fell on a line that brought the prickle of tears, but they did not fall:

"Fate comes when it will, and thus we are ready."

INTERVIEWER: Isn't a writer meant to have a sliver of ice in their heart?

NUNEZ: Yes, but not for the reader.

—SIGRID NUNEZ,
"The Art of Fiction no. 254," *The Paris Review*

ACKNOWLEDGMENTS

———

Thank you to Hafizah Geter and PJ Mark for being a more supportive and creatively generative team of agents than I could have dreamt of. Thank you to Hilary Redmon for a wonderfully inspiring and collaborative editing process, and to the whole team at Random House, especially Miriam Khanukaev, Ada Yonenaka, Barbara Bachman, Rachel Parker, and Jaylen Lopez. Thank you to Meghan O'Rourke and *The Yale Review* for publishing a first version of "Peering" and giving *Bibliophobia* a real start, and to everyone whose generosity and support made its completion possible: the Whiting Foundation; Dana Hawkes, Claire Reihill, and Mary Rhinelander at the T. S. Eliot House; and my forever colleagues, Bernard Schwartz, Sophie Herron, and Ricardo Maldonado for the precious time and encouragement.

In everything that came before and everything that came after: Becca Crawford and Merve Emre, I don't know where I'd be without you. I wouldn't have believed this could be a book without the early, necessarily forceful encouragement of

Ari Brostoff, Andrea Long Chu, Katherine Hill, and Namwali Serpell, who know better than I do what's best for me. Many brilliant friends stepped in along the way and helped me work through the writing, whether they knew it or not, including Sarah Ax, Elif Batuman, Lisa Goode Crawford, Nijah Cunningham, Katrina Dodson, Gloria Fisk, Moeko Fujii, Erica Goode, Briallen Hopper, Monica Huerta, Gina Patnaik, Juno Richards, Jeremy Schmidt, Dan Sinykin, Rachel Greenwald Smith, Jenny Xu, Irene and Gabe Yoon-Milner. Special thanks to Jesse McCarthy and Namwali Serpell for a last-minute stroke of editorial genius. Thanks to the New York family who saw me through some very weird times: Abigail Hawkins, Kristen Yoonsoo Kim, Mila Matveeva, Adam Moerder, Rachel Milano, Matt Morello, Leo Milano Morello, Jared Olmsted Salazar, Monica Salazar Olmsted, Kip Berman, and Cecily Swanson. Thank you to Aros, Braak, Enid, Nora, Nowhere, Wymar, and our indefatigable DM: there's no one I'd rather be trapped in Avernus with. Thank you to Swinton, who was with me through all of this. He was both the best worst cat and the worst best cat, and I miss him every day.

Thank you to all the Chihaya and Isojima family, especially my mother, Julie Chihaya. I wish my father, Frank Chihaya, could have seen this book's publication. He would have felt a lot of complicated things upon reading it, but foremost among them would have been pride.

Thank you to Christopher Shay, for teaching me to accept help, and—at least sometimes, even if grudgingly—how to simply accept.

ABOUT THE AUTHOR

SARAH CHIHAYA is a critic and essayist, and the recipient of a 2023 Whiting Creative Nonfiction Grant. Her work has appeared in *The New Yorker*, *The New York Review of Books*, *The Nation*, *New York* magazine, and *The Yale Review*, among other places, and she is the co-author of *The Ferrante Letters: An Experiment in Collective Criticism*. She lives in Queens, New York.

ABOUT THE TYPE

This book was set in Caslon, a typeface first designed in 1722 by William Caslon (1692–1766). Its widespread use by most English printers in the early eighteenth century soon supplanted the Dutch typefaces that had formerly prevailed. The roman is considered a "workhorse" typeface due to its pleasant, open appearance, while the italic is exceedingly decorative.